U.S. Armed Forces Abroad 1798-2007

U.S. ARMED FORCES ABROAD 1798-2007

RICHARD R. GRIMMETT
EDITOR

Nova Science Publishers, Inc.
New York

For permission to use material from this book please contact us:
Telephone 631-231-7269; Fax 631-231-8175
Web Site: http://www.novapublishers.com

LIBRARY OF CONGRESS CATALOGING-IN-PUBLICATION DATA

ISBN: 978-1-60692-722-9

Published by Nova Science Publishers, Inc. ✢ New York

CONTENTS

PREFACE

The President and Congress have historically played different roles when sending U.S. troops into hostile situations. The President has the power under Article II, Section 2, of the Constitution to use the armed forces to repel attacks. Congress under Article I, Section 8, has the power to declare war and raise and support the armed forces. The War Powers Resolution was enacted to ensure that the President and Congress share decisions where U.S. troops may become involved in hostilities. This sharing of power has often resulted in controversy, particularly when troops are sent into situations where there has not been a formal declaration of war. In most instances, Congress has used its legislative prerogatives through funding mechanisms or declarations of policy either to affirm or to place limits on presidential action. In three instances, Congress has authorized the use of military force in advance of hostilities: the Persian Gulf War (1991), military operations in Afghanistan (2001), and the "use of force against Iraq" resolution (2002). In each case, however, the President has maintained that while he may have sought congressional consultation and support, the President has the constitutional authority as Commander in Chief to use force, including the armed forces of the United States, to protect U.S. national security interests.

Chapter 1 – This article summarizes selected congressional votes related to instances in which U.S. Armed Forces have been sent abroad in potentially hostile situations. These votes reflect the type of congressional actions that observers maintain bear directly on issues affecting policy and the funding of troops abroad, often in the context of the War Powers Resolution, continued presence or withdrawal of troops, and the "use of force." The cases of Lebanon (1982-1983), Grenada (1983), Panama (1989), the Persian Gulf War (1990-1991), Somalia (1992-1995), Haiti (1993-1996), Bosnia (1992-1998), Kosovo (1999), the terrorist attack against America (2001) (including the use of U.S. Armed Forces in Afghanistan), and the use of U.S. Armed Forces against Iraq (2002-present) are examined. The roll call votes that are available online (since 1990 in the House and 1989 in the Senate) are linked.

Chapter 2 - This article lists hundreds of instances in which the United States has used its armed forces abroad in situations of military conflict or potential conflict or for other than normal peacetime purposes. It was compiled in part from various older lists and is intended primarily to provide a rough survey of past U.S. military ventures abroad, without reference to the magnitude of the given instance noted. The listing often contains references, especially from 1980 forward, to continuing military deployments especially U.S. military participation in multinational operations associated with NATO or the United Nations. Most of these post-1980 instances are summaries based on Presidential reports to Congress related to the War Powers Resolution. A comprehensive commentary regarding any of the instances listed is not undertaken here.

The instances differ greatly in number of forces, purpose, extent of hostilities, and legal authorization. Eleven times in its history the U.S. has formally declared war against foreign nations. These eleven U.S. war declarations encompassed five separate wars: the war with Great Britain declared in 1812, the war with Mexico declared in 1846, the War with Spain declared in 1898, the First World War, during which the U.S. declared war with Germany and with Austria-Hungary during 1917, World War II, during which the U.S. declared war against Japan, Germany, and Italy in 1941, and against Bulgaria, Hungary, and Rumania in 1942. Some of the instances were extended military engagements that might be considered undeclared wars. These include the Undeclared Naval War with France from 1798 to 1800; the First Barbary War from 1801 to 1805; the Second Barbary War of 1815; the Korean War of 1950-53; the Vietnam War from 1964 to 1973; the Persian Gulf War of 1991, global actions against foreign terrorists after the September 11, 2001 attacks on the United States, and the War with Iraq in 2003. With the exception of the Korean War, all of these conflicts received Congressional authorization in some form short of a formal declaration of war. Other, more recent instances often involve deployment of U.S. military forces as part of a multinational operation associated with NATO or the United Nations.

The majority of the instances listed prior to World War II were brief Marine or Navy actions to protect U.S. citizens or promote U.S. interests. A number were actions against pirates or bandits. Covert actions, disaster relief, and routine alliance stationing and training exercises are not included here, nor are the Civil and Revolutionary Wars and the continual use of U.S. military units in the exploration, settlement, and pacification of the Western part of the United States.

In: U.S. Armed Forces Abroad 1798-2007 ISBN 978-1-60692-722-9
Editor: Richard R. Grimmett, pp. 1-76

Chapter 1

U.S. ARMED FORCES ABROAD: SELECTED CONGRESSIONAL VOTES SINCE 1982*

Lisa Mages

SUMMARY

This article summarizes selected congressional votes related to instances in which U.S. Armed Forces have been sent abroad in potentially hostile situations. These votes reflect the type of congressional actions that observers maintain bear directly on issues affecting policy and the funding of troops abroad, often in the context of the War Powers Resolution, continued presence or withdrawal of troops, and the "use of force." The cases of Lebanon (1982-1983), Grenada (1983), Panama (1989), the Persian Gulf War (1990-1991), Somalia (1992-1995), Haiti (1993-1996), Bosnia (1992-1998), Kosovo (1999), the terrorist attack against America (2001) (including the use of U.S. Armed Forces in Afghanistan), and the use of U.S. Armed Forces against Iraq (2002-present) are examined. The roll call votes that are available online (since 1990 in the House and 1989 in the Senate) are linked.

* This is an edited, excerpted and augmented edition of a CRS Report for Congress publication, Order Code RL31693, dated September 7, 2007.

INTRODUCTION

The President and Congress have historically played different roles when sending U.S. troops into hostile situations. The President has the power under Article II, Section 2, of the Constitution to use the armed forces to repel attacks. Congress under Article I, Section 8, has the power to declare war and raise and support the armed forces. The War Powers Resolution[1] was enacted to ensure that the President and Congress share decisions where U.S. troops may become involved in hostilities.

This sharing of power has often resulted in controversy, particularly when troops are sent into situations where there has not been a formal declaration of war. In most instances, Congress has used its legislative prerogatives through funding mechanisms or declarations of policy either to affirm or to place limits on presidential action. In three instances, Congress has authorized the use of military force in advance of hostilities: the Persian Gulf War (1991), military operations in Afghanistan (2001), and the "use of force against Iraq" resolution (2002). In each case, however, the President has maintained that while he may have sought congressional consultation and support, the President has the constitutional authority as Commander in Chief to use force, including the armed forces of the United States, to protect U.S. national security interests.

CONTENT

This article describes the congressional debate that often surrounds the issue of employing the U.S. military abroad. Initially written in response to a congressional request for a list of votes on this topic from 1982-1992, this article has been updated as needed since that time. The votes included are those directly related to the use and funding of U.S. troops abroad, often in the context of the War Powers Resolution, or to their continued presence or withdrawal.

The laws, bills, and resolutions below are listed in the chronological order of the votes that were held. Links to the actual roll call votes are provided, when available (since 1990 in the House and 1989 in the Senate). These links include each Member's yea or nay vote.

[1] P.L. 93-148, November 7, 1973. For more detailed contextual and legislative history information, see CRS Report RL32267, The War Powers Resolution: After Thirty Years, by Richard F. Grimmett.

In some cases, House or Senate votes are voice votes, and, thus, no roll call vote exists. Moreover, the ultimate disposition of amendments listed in the article (i.e., whether such amendments were incorporated into any final law) may not be self- evident. In other instances, only one chamber of Congress may have voted on a particular measure; for example, a House or Senate simple resolution is a nonlegislative measure that expresses nonbinding opinions on policies or issues and is effective only in the chamber in which it is proposed. It does not require concurrence by the other chamber or approval by the President.

LEBANON (1982-1983)

On September 29, 1982, President Reagan deployed 1,200 marines to serve as part of a multinational observer force to restore the sovereignty of the Lebanese government. By March 30, 1984, the mission had ended.

Congress	Bill and Title	Description and Comments	Votes
98th	**S. 639 (P.L. 98-43)** Lebanon Emergency Assistance Act of 1983	Required the President to seek statutory authority for any substantial expansion of U.S. participation in the multinational peacekeeping force in Lebanon.	Measure passed Senate May 20, 1983 (voice vote) Measure passed House June 2, 1983 276-76 (vote #153)
	H.J.Res. 364 Multinational Force in Lebanon Resolution	To provide statutory authority under the War Powers Resolution for continued U.S. participation in the multinational peacekeeping force in Lebanon for up to 18 months after enactment.	Measure passed House September 28, 1983 270-161 (vote #356)

Table.Continued

Congress	Bill and Title	Description and Comments	Votes
	H.Amdt. 395 to H.J.Res. 364	Long substitute amendment requires the President to invoke the War Powers Resolution by the end of November, or at the end of any month thereafter, unless President certifies to Congress that a cease-fire was in effect and being observed by all parties, and that significant progress was being made in negotiations to broaden the base of Lebanese government.	Rejected in House September 28, 1983 158-272 (vote #360)
	S.J.Res. 159 (P.L. 98-119) Multinational Force in Lebanon Resolution	Authorizes the President to maintain U.S. Armed Forces in Lebanon as part of a multinational peacekeeping force for 18 months; determines that the requirements of Section 4(a)(1) of the War Powers Resolution became operational on August 29, 1983.	Measure passed House September 29, 1983 253-156 (vote #370) Measure passed Senate September 29, 1983 54-46 (vote #274)
	S.Amdt. 2231 to S.J.Res. 159	Baker motion to kill the Byrd amendment stating that U.S. Marines in Lebanon became engaged in hostilities on August 29, 1983, requiring the President to submit report to Congress under Section 4(a)(1) of the War Powers Resolution concerning hostilities, and extending for 60 days from enactment of the resolution the President's authority to keep U.S. forces in Lebanon.	Agreed to in Senate September 29, 1983 55-45 (vote #269)

	S.Amdt. 2228 to S.J.Res. 159	Baker motion to kill the Pell amendment to authorize the U.S. Marines to remain in Lebanon for an additional six months instead of 18.	Agreed to in Senate September 29, 1983 62-38 (vote #270)
	S.Amdt. 2239 to S.J.Res. 159	Baker motion to kill the Tsongas amendment stating that a purpose of the deployment of U.S. Marines in Lebanon was to help the Lebanese government "maintain a secure area from which to restore full control over its own territory."	Agreed to in Senate September 29, 1983 56-42 (vote #271)
	S.Amdt. 2240 to S.J.Res. 159	Baker motion to kill the Levin amendment stating that "actual or imminent hostilities involving U.S. armed forces" began on August 29, 1983.	Agreed to in Senate September 29, 1983 54-45 (vote #272)
	S.Amdt. 2233 to S.J.Res. 159	Baker motion to kill Eagleton amendment to allow the U.S. to take such "defensive measures as may be appropriate" to protect the multinational peacekeeping force in Lebanon rather than "protective" measures; would require the President to report to Congress periodically on the results of efforts to secure removal of all foreign forces from Lebanon.	Agreed to in Senate September 29, 1983 66-34 (vote #273)
	H.Amdt. 494 to H.R. 4185 Department of Defense Appropriations for FY1984	Long amendment to prohibit funds for deployment of U.S. Armed Forces participating in the multinational peacekeeping force in Lebanon after March 1, 1984.	Rejected in House November 2, 1983 153-274 (vote #441)

GRENADA (1983)

On October 25, 1983, President Reagan sent U.S. Marines and Army troops to Grenada in order to protect American lives and restore law and order at the request of the Organization of Eastern Caribbean States. All U.S. troops were removed from Grenada by December 15, 1983.

Congress	Bill and Title	Description and Comments	Votes
98th	**S.Amdt. 2462 to H.J.Res. 308** (P.L. 98-161) Joint resolution increasing the statutory limit on the public debt	Hart amendment to invoke the War Powers Resolution with respect to American military involvement in Grenada.	Agreed to in Senate October 28, 1983 64-20 (vote #321)
	H.J.Res. 402	Declared that the requirements of Section 4(a)(1) of the War Powers Resolution became operative on October 25, 1983, when U.S. armed forces were introduced into Grenada.	Measure passed House November 1, 1983 403-23 (vote #437)

PANAMA (1989)

On December 20, 1989, President George H.W. Bush deployed 14,000 U.S. military forces to Panama in order to protect American lives, restore Panamanian democracy, and apprehend General Manuel Noriega. Congress did not immediately react to the situation, as the 101st Congress, first session had ended on November 22, 1989; the second session of the 101st Congress did not begin until January 23, 1990. The 14,000 U.S. troops were removed from Panama by February 13, 1990.

Congress	Bill and Title	Description and Comments	Votes
101st	**H.Con.Res. 262**	Expresses sadness over the loss of U.S. soldiers' lives as a result of Operation Just Cause and commends the President for his efforts to provide for the early return of the remaining U.S. troops from Panama.	Measure agreed to in House February 7, 1990 389-26 (vote #12)

PERSIAN GULF WAR (1990-1991)

On August 2, 1990, Iraqi troops invaded Kuwait, seized its oil fields, ousted the Kuwaiti leadership, installed a new government in Kuwait City, and massed troops on the Saudi Arabian border. On August 9, President Bush reported that he had deployed U.S. troops to the region. Legislation in late 1990 (101st Congress, second session) focused on imposing sanctions against Iraq, in seeking the withdrawal of Iraqi forces from the area, and in supporting the President in carrying out the provisions of the relevant United Nations Security Council resolutions. On January 12, 1991 (102nd Congress, first session), the Congress authorized the "use of force" against Iraq in advance of the outbreak of hostilities with Iraq on January 16.

Congress	Bill and Title	Description and Comments	Votes
101st	**S.Res. 318** Resolution to condemn Iraq's invasion of Kuwait	Commends the President for his initial actions with respect to Iraq. Urges the President to seek ... additional multilateral actions involving air, sea, or land forces as necessary to maintain or restore international peace or security.	Measure agreed to in Senate August 2, 1990 97-0 (vote #211)

Table. Continued

Congress	Bill and Title	Description and Comments	Votes
	H.J.Res. 658 United States Policy on Iraqi Aggression Resolution	Supports the deployment of U.S. armed forces to the Persian Gulf region and expresses appreciation to such forces.	Measure passed House October 1, 1990 380-29 (vote #394)
101st	**S.Con.Res. 147**	Supports continued action by the President to deter Iraqi aggression and to protect American lives and interests in the region.	Measure agreed to in Senate October 2, 1990 96-3 (vote #258)
102nd	**H.J.Res. 77 (P.L. 102-1)** Authorization for Use of Military Force Against Iraq Resolution	Joint resolution to authorize the use of United States armed forces pursuant to United Nations Security Council Resolution 678.	Measure passed House January 12, 1991 250-183 (vote #9)
	H.Con.Res. 32	Finds that the Constitution vests all power to declare war in the Congress. Declares that any offensive action against Iraq must be explicitly approved in advance by the Congress.	Measure agreed to in House January 12, 1991 302-131 (vote #7)

	H.Con.Res. 33	Authorizes the continued use of American military force to enforce the United Nations economic embargo against Iraq, to defend Saudi Arabia from direct Iraqi attack, and to protect American forces in the region. Declares that (1) the Constitution requires the President to obtain authorization from the Congress before initiating new offensive military action or waging war against Iraq or Iraqi forces and (2) the Congress does not rule out the enactment at a later time of a declaration of war or other congressional authorization for the use of force.	Measure rejected in House January 12, 1991 183-250 (vote #8)

Table. Continued

Congress	Bill and Title	Description and Comments	Votes
	S.J.Res. 1	Authorizes the use of American military force to enforce the United Nations economic embargo against Iraq, defend Saudi Arabia from direct Iraqi attack, and protect American forces in the region. Declares that (1) the Constitution vests all power to declare war in the Congress and (2) the Congress will expeditiously consider any presidential request for a declaration of war or for authority to use military force against Iraq.	Measure rejected by Senate January 12, 1991 46-53 (vote #1)
	S.J.Res. 2 Authorization for Use of Military Force Against Iraq Resolution	Authorizes the President to use U.S. armed forces against Iraq pursuant to United Nations Security Council Resolution 678.	Measure passed Senate January 12, 1991 52-4 (vote #2)

SOMALIA (1992-1995)

On December 10, 1992, President Bush reported that he had deployed U.S. troops into Somalia on December 8, in response to United Nations Security Council Resolution 794, which authorized the Secretary General to "use all necessary means to establish as soon as possible a secure environment for humanitarian relief operations in Somalia" and to provide military forces for accomplishing this. U.S. troops were deployed to assist United Nations Forces in Somalia (UNOSOM) throughout 1993 and 1994, ending on March 3, 1995.

Congress	Bill and Title	Description and Comments	Votes
103rd	**S.J.Res. 45**	Joint resolution authorizing the use of United States Armed Forces in Somalia pursuant to United Nations Security Council Resolution 794 providing for a secure environment to deliver relief supplies into Somalia. The House reported version authorized U.S. troops under the War Powers Resolution, but terminated such authorization at the earlier of (1) end of one year from date of enactment of the act unless extended by Congress; or (2) expiration of the United Nations-led force in Somalia.	Measure passed Senate February 4, 1993 (voice vote) Measure passed House May 25, 1993 243-179 (vote #183)
	H.Amdt. 66 to S.J.Res. 45	Gilman substitute amendment to reduce from one year to six months authorization for U.S. participation and to delete the section of the bill complying with the War Powers Resolution.	Rejected in House May 25, 1993 179-248 (vote #179)
	H.Amdt. 67 to S.J.Res. 45	Roth amendment to end the U.S. troop authorization and financial aid in Somalia on June 30, 1993.	Rejected in House May 25, 1993 127-299 (vote #180)
	H.Amdt. 68 to S.J.Res. 45	Solomon amendment to commend U.S. Armed Forces for esta b lishing a secure environment for humanitarian relief in Somalia.	Agreed to in House May 25, 1993 425-0 (vote #181)

Table. Continued

Congress	Bill and Title	Description and Comments	Votes
	H.Amdt. 68 to S.J.Res. 45	Separate vote at request of Walker on amendment adopted by Solomon in Committee of the Whole to commend U.S. forces for establishing a secure environment for humanitarian relief in Somalia.	Agreed to in House May 25, 1993 419-0 (vote #182)
	S.Amdt. 790 to S.1298 National Defense Authorizati on Act for Fiscal Year 1994	Byrd amendment to the Byrd amendment expressing sense of Senate that the President should outline goals, objectives, and duration of deployment of U.S. troops in Somalia and report to Congress by October 15, 1993; President should ask for and receiv e cong ressional authorization for continued deployment in Somalia by November 15, 1993; U.S. participation would terminate if Congress failed to authorize such continued involvement.	Agreed to in Senate September 9, 1993 90-7 (vote #252)
	H.R. 2401 (P.L. 103-160) National Defense Authorizati on Act for FY1994		Measure passed House September 29, 1993 268-162 (vote #474)
			Measure passed Senate October 6, 1993 (voice vote)

	H.Amdt. 319 to H.R. 2401	Gephardt amendment requiring the President to report to Congress by October 15, 1993, on goals, objectives, and duration of U.S. Armed Forces in Somalia and expressing sense of Congress that the President should seek congressional authorization by November 15, 1993, for continued deployment in Somalia.	Agreed to in House September 28, 1993 406-26 (vote #463)
	H.Amdt. 319 to H.R. 2401	Separate vote at request of Walker on Gephardt amendment adopted in the Committee of the Whole (described above).	Agreed to in House September 29, 1993 405-23 (vote #472)
		Spence motion to recommit bill to House Armed Services with instructions to report back with amendment requiring the President to certify that it is vital and necessary to protect U.S. national interests before placing U.S. troops under control of a foreign national on behalf of the United Nations.	Rejected in House September 29, 1993 192-238 (vote #473)
	H.R. 3116 (P.L. 103-139) Department of Defense Appropriati ons for FY1994		Measure passed Senate October 21, 1993 (voice vote)

Table. Continued

Congress	Bill and Title	Description and Comments	Votes
		Thurmond motion to kill McCain amendment (S.Amdt. 1043) to prohibit funding of U.S. military operations in Somalia except for withdrawal of all U.S. troops.	Agreed to in Senate October 15, 1993 61-38 (vote #313)
	S.Amdt. 1042 to H.R.3116	Byrd amendment to prohibit funding of U.S. military operations in Somalia after March 31, 1994, except for limited purposes if the President requests and Congress authorizes an extension; requires U.S. forces to be under command of U.S. commanders.	Agreed to in Senate October 15, 1993 76-23 (vote #314)
	H.Con.Res. 170	Concurrent resolution directing the President pursuant to Section 5(c) of the War Powers Resolution to remove United States Armed Forces from Somalia by January 31, 1994.	Measure agreed to in House November 9, 1993 (voice vote)
	H.Amdt. 384 to H.Con.Res. 170	Gilman amendment to change deadline for removal of U.S. troops in Somalia from March 31, 1994, to January 31, 1994.	Agreed to in House 224-203 November 9, 1993 (vote #555)
	H.Amdt. 385 to H.Con.Res. 170	Hamilton substitute amendment to change deadline for removal of U.S. troops back to March 31, 1994, from January 31, 1994; substituted by Gilman.	Agreed to in House 226-201 November 9, 1993 (vote #556)

	H.R. 3759 (P.L. 103-211) Emergency Supplemen-tal Appropriati ons Act for FY1994		Measure passed House February 3, 1994 337-74 (vote #13) Measure passed Senate February 10, 1994 85-10 (vote #45)
	H.Amdt. 424 to H.R. 3759	Frank amendment to delete $1.2 billion for peacekeeping and humanitarian assistance in Somalia, Bosnia, Iraq, and Haiti.	Rejected in House February 3, 1994 158-260 (vote #8)
	S.Amdt. 1453 to H.R. 3759	Feingold amendment to eliminate $1.2 billion for peacekeeping operations in Somalia, Bosnia, Iraq, and Haiti.	Rejected in Senate February 10, 1994 19-76 (vote #40)
	H.R. 4650 (P.L. 103-335) Department of Defense Appropriati ons for FY1995		Measure passed Senate August 11, 1994 86-14 (vote #282)
	S.Amdt. 2538 to H.R. 4650	K emp thorne amendment prohibiting funds from supporting the continued presence of U.S. troops in Somalia after September 30, 1994.	Agreed to in Senate August 10, 1994 54-44 (vote #278)

HAITI (1993-1 996)

On October 20, 1993, President Clinton reported that U.S. ships had begun enforcing a United Nations embargo against Haiti. On September 19, 1994, President Clinton had deployed 1,500 troops to Haiti to restore democracy; that level was ultimately increased to over 20,000. By March 21, 1995, U.S. troops were reduced to under 5,300 and incorporated into the United Nations Multinational Force in Haiti. By September 21, 1995, they were reduced to under 2,500 personnel. U.S.

Congress	Bill and Title	Description and Comments	Votes
103rd	**H.R. 3116 (P.L. 103-139)** Department of Defense Appropriations for FY1994		Measure passed Senate October 21, 1993 (voice vote)
	S.Amdt. 1072 to H.R. 3116	Helms amendment to prohibit funding any U.S. military operations in Haiti unless Congress explicitly authorizes such action or the President certifies to Congress that U.S. citizens are in danger.	Rejected in Senate October 21, 1993 19-81 (vote #321)
	S.Amdt. 1074 to H.R. 3116	Mitchell amendment expressing sense of Congress that Congress should authorize all U.S. military operations in Haiti unless U.S. citizens are in imminent need of protection and evacuation or that deployment is vital to national security	Agreed to in Senate October 21, 1993 98-2 (vote #322)

		interests.	
	H.R. 3759 (P.L. 103-211) Emergency Supplemental Appropriations Act for FY1994		Measure passed House February 3, 1994 337-74 (vote #13) Measure passed Senate February 10, 1994 85-10 (vote #45)
	H.Amdt. 424 to H.R. 3759	Frank amendment deleting $1.2 billion for peacekeeping and humanitarian assistance in Haiti, Bosnia, Somalia, and Iraq.	Rejected in House February 3, 1994 158-260 (vote #8)
	S.Amdt. 1453 to H.R. 3759	F e ing o ld am endm en t eliminating $1.2 billion for peacekeeping operations in Haiti, Bosnia, Somalia, and Iraq.	Rejected in Senate February 10, 1994 19-76 (vote #40)
	H.R. 4301 National Defense Authorization Act for FY1995		Measure passed House June 9, 1994 260-158 (vote #226)
	H.Amdt. 575 to H.R. 4301	Substitute amendment to the Goss amendment (see below) sought to express the sense of Congress that the U.S. should not attack Haiti except in a case of a clear and present danger.	Rejected in House May 24, 1994 191-236 (vote #196)

Table. Continued

Congress	Bill and Title	Description and Comments	Votes
	H.Amdt. 574 to H.R. 4301	Goss amendment expressing sense of Congress that the United States with the Organization of American States (OAS) and the United Nations should establish a safe haven for Haitian refugees on Ile de la Gonava; establish legitimate Haitian administration to govern; the President should not undertake any military action against Haiti unless it presents a clear and present danger to the United States.	Agreed to in House May 24, 1994 223-201 (vote #197)
	H.Amdt. 574 to H.R. 4301	Separate vote at request of Dellums on the amendment offered by Goss, previously voted on at roll call vote #197 above.	Rejected in House June 9, 1994 195-226 (vote #224)
	H.R. 4426 (P.L. 103-306) Foreign Operations, Export Financing, and Related Programs Appropriations for FY1995		Measure passed Senate July 15, 1994 84-9 (vote #203)
	S.Amdt. 2117	Gregg amendment to	Rejected in

	to H.R. 4426	prohibit military action in Haiti unless the operations are authorized in advance by Congress or necessary to protect U.S. citizens for national security interests.	Senate June 29, 1994 34-65 (vote #172)
	S.Amdt. 2118 to H.R. 4426	Mitchell amendment expressing sense of Congress that Congress should authorize all U.S. military operations in Haiti unless U.S. citizens are in immediate need of protection or deployment is vital to U.S. national security.	Agreed to in Senate June 29, 1994 93-4 (vote #173)
	H.R. 4624 (P.L. 103-327) Department of Veterans Affairs Appropriations for FY1995		Measure passed Senate August 4, 1994 86-9 (vote #262)
	S.Amdt. 2445 to H.R. 4624	Dole amendment expressing sense of Senate that United Nations Security Council Resolution 940 did not constitute authorization for deployment of U.S. forces in Haiti under the Constitution or the War Powers Resolution.	Agreed to in Senate August 3, 1994 100-0 (vote #254)

Table. Continued

Congress	Bill and Title	Description and Comments	Votes
	H.R. 4606 {P.L. 103-333) Departments of Labor, Health and Human Services, and Education Appropriations for FY1995	McCain motion to kill Specter amendment (S.Amdt. 2460) barring the President from deploying U.S. troops to restore legitimately elected Haitian government unless authorized by Congress, unless vital to national security interests, or to protect lives of U.S. citizens.	Agreed to in Senate August 5, 1994 63-31 (vote #263)
	H.Con.Res. 290	C oncurre n t r e solution commending the President and the special delegation to Haiti; supporting U.S. Armed Forces in Haiti; supporting an orderly withdrawal of U.S. forces as soon as possible.	Measure agreed to in House September 19, 1994 353-45 (vote #424)
	S.Res. 259	Resolution expressing sense of the Senate supporting U.S. forces in Haiti; commending the special delegation led by former President Carter; supporting lifting of economic sanctions on Haiti; supporting prompt and orderly withdrawal of all U.S. forces.	Measure agreed to in Senate September 21, 1994 94-5 (vote #301)
	S.J.Res. 229 (P.L. 103-423) Joint resolution regarding	Joint resolution expressing sense of Congress for a prompt and orderly withdrawal of all U.S.	Measure passed Senate October 6, 1994 91-8 (vote #323)

	United States policy toward Haiti	forces from Haiti as soon as possible; requires President to submit reports to Congress on the scope and duration of U.S. mission in Haiti.	Measure passed House October 7, 1994 (voice vote)
	H.J.Res. 416 Limited Authorization for the United States-led Force in Haiti Resolution	Joint resolution expressing sense of Congress that all U.S. troops should be promptly and orderly withdrawn from Haiti as soon as possible; President should have sought congressional approval before deployment of troops; requires the President to submit statement of national security objectives of Operation Uphold Democracy within seven days of enactment.	Measure passed House October 7, 1994 236-182 (vote #500)
	H.Amdt. 922 to H.J.Res. 416	Gilman amendment expressing sense of Congress that President should not have ordered U.S. troops to occupy Haiti and should immediately begin the "safe and orderly withdrawal" of all U.S. forces; provides for consideration of joint resolution to be introduced January 3, 1995, which if enacted, would prohibit continued use of U.S. troops in Haiti within 30 days.	Rejected in House October 6, 1994 205-225 (vote #497)

Table. Continued

Congress	Bill and Title	Description and Comments	Votes
	H.Amdt. 923 to H.J.Res. 416	Dellums amendment expressing sense of Congress that all U.S. troops should be promptly and orderly withdrawn from Haiti; President should have sought congressional approval before deploying troops; requires President to submit to Congress within seven days of enactment a statement on national security objectives of Operation Uphold Democracy and other reports on situation there.	Agreed to in House October 6, 1994 258-167 (vote #498)
	H.Amdt. 924 to H.J.Res. 416	Toricelli amendment authorizing the presence of U.S. troops in Haiti until March 1, 1995, unless President determines and certifies to Congress that continued presence is essential to protect U.S. citizens or vital to national security interests.	Rejected in House October 7, 1994 27-398 (vote #499)

Bosnia (1992-1998)

The civil war in the former Yugoslav Republic of Bosnia-Herzegovina resulted in U.S. military participation in various efforts over several years to halt the fighting. The United States participated in both United Nations and NATO actions without explicit congressional authorization. Beginning in 1992, the

United Nations Security Council adopted Resolution 770, which called on all nations to take "all measures necessary" to facilitate the delivery of humanitarian assistance to Sarajevo. On August 11, 1992, the Senate passed S.Res. 330, which urged the President to work for such a resolution and pledged funds for participation, but also said that no U.S. military personnel should be introduced into hostilities without clearly defined objectives.

On the same day, the House passed H.Res. 554, which urged the Security Council to authorize measures, including the use of force, to ensure humanitarian relief. As the conflict in Bosnia continued and escalated over the next several years, U.S. troops were sent to participate in NATO and United Nations peacekeeping missions. Consequently, leaders in Congress began calling for greater congressional involvement in decisions.

In 1994, for example, the Senate passed S. 2042, which called for the United States to end unilaterally its arms embargo with Bosnia; the Senate also passed an amendment to S. 2042 which stated that no ground combat troops should be deployed to Bosnia unless previously authorized by Congress. The House did not act on the measure. With the signing of the Dayton Peace Agreement for Bosnia on December 14, 1995, NATO took over the ground operation from UNPROFOR (United Nations Protection Force). Consequently, in late 1995, over 20,000 U.S. combat troops were sent to Bosnia as part of the NATO-led peacekeeping force. In December 1995, Congress considered and voted on a number of bills and resolutions, but the House and Senate could not come to consensus on any single measure. In 1996, President Clinton agreed to provide up to 8,500 ground troops to participate in the NATO-led follow-on force in Bosnia termed the Stabilization Force (SFOR).

Subsequent efforts by both the House and Senate to require the President to either limit funding for the Bosnia operations or to bring the troops home did not succeed. On March 18, 1998, for example, the House defeated by a vote of 193-225 H.Con.Res. 227, which would have directed the President to remove U.S. Armed Forces from the Republic of Bosnia- Herzegovina, pursuant to Section 5(c) of the War Powers Resolution.

On July 22, 2002, President Bush reported to Congress that U.S. Armed Forces contributions to SFOR in Bosnia-Herzegovina were approximately 2,400 personnel.

Congress	Bill and Title	Description and Comments	Votes
102nd	**S.Res. 330**	Expresses the sense of the Senate that the President should call upon the United Nations to authorize all means, including multinational military action, to ensure the flow of humanitarian relief in Bosnia-Herzegovina and to gain access for the U.N. and International Red Cross personnel to refugee and war camps.	Measure agreed to in Senate August 11, 1992 74-22 (vote #186)
	S.Amdt. 2925 to S.Res. 330	Warner amendment to express the Senate's support for the six measures that President Bush said on August 6 that the Administration was taking to help resolve the Balkan Crisis.	Agreed to in Senate August 10, 1992 90-5 (vote #184)
	S.Amdt. 2929 to S.Res. 330	Stevens amendment to express the sense of the Senate that the United States will provide necessary funds for U.S. participation in humanitarian and multilateral military action in Bosnia-Herzegovina as mandated by the United Nations.	Agreed to in Senate August 11, 1992 82-13 (vote #185)
103rd	**H.R. 3116 (P.L. 103-139) Department of Defense Appropriations Act, 1994**	Making appropriations for the Department of Defense for the fiscal year ending September 30, 1994.	Measure passed House September 30, 1993 325-102 (vote #480) Senate agreed to conference

			report November 10, 1993 88-9 (vote #368)
	S.Amdt. 1073 to H.R. 3116	Mitchell amendment to express the sense of Congress that none of the funds in the bill should be used to deploy U.S. troops in Bosnia-Herzegovina unless authorized by Congress, except for humanitarian missions started before October 20, 1993.	Agreed to in Senate October 20, 1993 99-1 (vote #320)
	S. 2042	A bill to remove the United States arms embargo of the g o ve r n m e nt of Bosnia-Herzegovina.	Measure passed Senate May 12, 1994 (voice vote)
	S.Amdt. 1696 to S. 2042	Mitchell amendment to direct the President to seek the immediate agreement of NATO allies to terminate the arms e m barg o ag ainst Bosnia-Herzegovina, direct the President to seek a U.N. Security Council resolution to terminate the arms embargo and ... authorize U.S. air power to implement NATO exclusion zones and to protect U.N. forces, but prohibit the deployment of U.S. ground combat forces without congressional authorization.	Agreed to in Senate May 10, 1994 50-49 (vote #110)

Table. Continued

Congress	Bill and Title	Description and Comments	Votes
103rd	**S.Amdt. 1695 to S. 2042**	Dole amendment to require the President to terminate the U.S. arm s em barg o of Bosnia-Herzegovina upon receipt of a request from that government for assistance in its right of self-defense and to prohibit interference with the transfer of conventional arms by the executive branch. The amendment also states that nothing in the amendment shall e interpretedasanauthorization for the deployment of U.S. forces.	Agreed to in Senate May 12, 1994 50-49 (vote #111)
104th	**H.R. 2076** Departments of Commerce, Justice, and State, the Judiciary, and Related Agencies Appropriations Act, 1996	Making appropriations for the Departments of Commerce, Justice, and State, the Judiciary, and related agencies for the fiscal year ending September 30, 1996, and for other purposes.	Measure passed House July 26, 1995 272-151 (vote #585) Measure passed Senate September 29, 1995 (voice vote) House adopted conference report December 6, 1995 256-166 (vote #841) Senate adopted conference report December 7, 1995 50-48 (vote #591) Vetoed by President December 19, 1995 House failed

			to override veto January 3, 1996 240-159 (vote #4)
104th	**S.Amdt. 2842 to H.R. 2076**	Gregg amendment to express the sense of the Senate that U.S. troops should not be deployed to Bosnia-Herzegovina unless Congress approves the deployment or the temporary deployment as necessary to evacuate U.N. peacekeeping forces from imminent danger, to undertake air rescue operations, or to provide humanitarian supplies.	Agreed to in Senate September 29, 1995 94-2 (vote #479)
	H.Res. 247	Expresses the sense of the House of Representatives to the deployment of the United States armed forces on the ground in the territory of the Republic of Bosnia-Herzegovina to enforce a peace agreement. Gilman motion to suspend the rules and adopt the resolution ... that a successful outcome for the Bosnia peace talks should not assume the deployment of U.S. troops, and that any deployment should be authorized by Congress.	Measure agreed to in House October 30, 1995 315-103 (vote #745)

Table. Continued

Congress	Bill and Title	Description and Comments	Votes
	H.R. 2606	To prohibit the use of funds appropriated to the Department of Defense from being used for the deployment on the ground of U.S. Armed Forces in the Republ ic of Bosnia-Herzegovina as part of any peacekeeping operations, or as part of any implementation force, unless funds for such deployment are specifically appropriated by law.	Measure passed House November 17, 1995 243-171 (vote #814) Measure rejected in Senate December 13, 1995 22-77 (vote #601)
	H.R. 2770	To prohibit federal funds from being used for the deployment on the ground of U.S. Armed Forces in the Republic of Bosnia-Herzegovina as part of any peacekeeping operations, or as part of any implementation force.	Measure rejected in House December 13, 1995 210-218 (vote #856)
104th	**H.Res. 302**	Relating to the deployment of the U.S. Armed Forces in and around the territory of the Republic o f Bosnia-Herzegovina to enforce the peace agreement between the parties to the conflict. Declares that the House has serious concerns and opposes the President's policy to deploy U.S. ground troops to Bosnia ... and that the U.S. government should be impartial and evenhanded with all parties in the Bosnian conflict as necessary to ensure the safety of U.S. troops.	Measure agreed to in House December 13, 1995 287-141 (vote #857)
	S.Con.Res 35	A concurrent resolution expressing the opposition of the Congress to President Clinton's	Measure rejected in Senate

		planned deployment of United States ground forces to Bosnia wh ile also expressing congressional support for the U.S. troops ordered by the President to help implement the Bosnia peace agreement.	December 13, 1995 47-52 (vote #602)
	H.Res. 306	Expressing the sense of the House of Representatives that while some Members of Congress have questions and concerns about the deployment of U.S. Armed Forces to Bosn i a , the House unequivocally supports the men and women of the U.S. Armed Forces who are serving there.	Measure rejected in House December 14, 1995 190-237 (vote #858)
104th	**S.J.Res. 44**	A joint resolution expressing support for U.S. troops in Bosnia, but expressing reservations about the deployment of such troops. The measure would also limit the deployment to "approximately" one year and require the President to limit the use of U.S. troops in Bosnia to the enforcement of the military provisions of the peace agreement and provide an exit strategy from Bosnia that would include an international effort to achieve a military balance in Bosnia by arming the federation of Bosnia.	Measure passed Senate December 14, 1995 69-30 (vote #603)

Table. Continued

Congress	Bill and Title	Description and Comments	Votes
105th	**H.R. 1119 (P.L. 105-85)** National Defense Authorization Act for Fiscal Year 1998	Anact to authorize appropriations for FY1998 for military activities of the Department of Defense ... and for other purposes.	Measure passed House, June 25, 1997 304-120 (vote #236) Measure passed Senate July 11, 1997 (unanimous consent) House adopted conference report October 28, 1997 286-123 (vote #534) Senate adopted conference report November 6, 1997 90-10 (vote #296)
105th	**H.Amdt. 204 to H.R. 1119**	Hilleary substitute amendment to the Buyer amendment to prohibit the obligation of funds for ground deployment of U.S. troops in Bosnia after December 31, 1997, unless the President submits a report to Congress requesting an extension of funding. The Hilleary amendment would require the extension to be approved by a joint resolution of Congress and would permit	Rejected in House June 24, 1997 196-231 (vote #233)

		deployment for an additional 180 days or until June 30, 1998.	
	H.Amdt. 203 to H.R. 1119	Buyer amendment to prohibit funding for U.S. ground troops in Bosnia after June 30, 1998.	Agreed to in House June 24, 1997 278-148 (vote #234)
	S. 936 National Defense Authorization Act for Fiscal Year 1998	Expresses the sense of Congress that U.S. troops should pull out of Bosnia by June 30, 1998.	Measure passed Senate July 11, 1997 94-4 (vote #173)
105th	**H.R. 2266 (P.L. 105-56)** Department of Defense Appropriations Act, 1998	Making appropriations for the Department of Defense for the fiscal year ending September 30, 1998, and for other purposes. The bill/conference report would cut off funding for U.S. troops in Bosnia after June 30, 1998, but would permit the President to request further funding.	Measure passed House July 29, 1997 322-105 (vote #338) Measure passed Senate July 29, 1997 (unanimous consent) House agreed to conference report September 25, 1997 56-65 (vote #442) Senate agreed to conference report September 25, 1997 93-5 (vote #258)

Table. Continued

Congress	Bill and Title	Description and Comments	Votes
			Became P.L. 105-56 October 8, 1997
			Line item veto by the President October 21, 1997
	H.Con.Res 227 Bosnia and Herzegovina U.S. Troop Removal bill	Directed the President, pursuant to Section 5(c) of the War Powers Resolution, to remove U.S. Armed Forces from the Rep ublic of Bosnia-Herzegovina.	Measure rejected in House March 18, 1998 193-225 (vote #58)
	S.Amdt. 2316 to Treaty 105-36 Protocols to the NATO Treaty of 1949 on Accession of Poland, Hungary, and Czech Republic	Craig amendment to add language to the resolution of ratification that would require Congress and the President to enact legislation specifically authorizing the continued deployment of U.S. troops in Bosnia before the United States ratifies the NATO expansion treaty.	Rejected in Senate April 30, 1998 20-80 (vote #110)
105th	**S.Amdt. 2328 to Treaty 105-36** Protocols to the NATO Treaty of 1949 on Accession of Poland, Hungary, and Czech Republic	B. Smith amendment to add language to the resolution of ratification that would require both houses of Congress to vote on legislation, prior to ratification of N A T O expansion, that would authorize continued U.S. troop deployments to Bosnia.	Rejected in Senate April 30, 1998 16-83 (vote #116)

	H.R. 3616 (P.L. 105-261) Strom Thurmond National Defense Authorization Act for Fiscal Year 1999	Frank motion to recommit the bill to the National Security Committee with instructions to report it back with an amendment that no funds appropriated for the Department of Defense for FY1999 may be used for the deployment of U.S. Armed Forces in the Republic of Bosnia-Herzegovina after December 31, 1998, unless a law has been enacted that explicitly authorizes the deployment of such armed forces.	Rejected in House May 21, 1998 167-251 (vote #182)
	S. 2057 National Defense Authorization Act for Fiscal Year 1999	An original bill to authorize appropriations for FY1999 for military activities of the Department of Defense ... and for other purposes.	Measure passed Senate June 25, 1998 88-4 (vote #181)
	S.Amdt. 2975 to S. 2057	Thurmond amendment to express the sense of Congress that U.S. ground forces should not remain in Bosnia indefinitely, and that the President should work with NATO to withdraw U.S. forces "within a reasonable period of time."	Agreed to in Senate June 24, 1998 90-5 (vote #170)
	S.Amdt. 2977 to S. 2057	McCain motion to table (kill) the Smith amendment that would prohibit funding for U.S. ground troop deployment in Bosnia if both houses of Congress do not vote by March 31, 1999, on legislation that would authorize continued deployment in Bosnia.	Agreed to in Senate June 24, 1998 65-31 (vote #171)

Table. Continued

Congress	Bill and Title	Description and Comments	Votes
105th	**S. 2132** Department of Defense Appropriations Act, 1999	An original bill making appropriations f or the Department of Defense for the fiscal year ending September 30, 1999 ... and for other purposes.	Indefinitely postponed in the Senate July 30, 1998 (unanimous consent)
		McCain motion to table (kill) the Hutchison amendment (S.Amdt. 3413) that would require the President to reduce U.S. combat forces in Bosnia to 6,500 by February 2, 1999, and by 5,000 by October 1, 1999.	Agreed to in Senate July 30, 1998 68-31 (vote #249)

Kosovo (1999)

On March 24, 1999, President Clinton ordered U.S. military forces to begin air strikes against the Federal Republic of Yugoslavia (Serbia and Montenegro) in cooperation with the NATO-led operation. The strike was ordered in response to Yugoslavia's campaign of violence against ethnic Albanians in the province of Kosovo. On June 3, 1999, Yugoslavia agreed to a peace plan calling for withdrawal of Yugoslav forces from Kosovo to include an international peacekeeping force. On June 10, 1999, NATO air strikes were halted, and Yugoslav forces withdrew their military forces from Kosovo by June 20, 1999.

Congress, while not authorizing directly, and in advance, this military action, introduced and voted on several legislative measures related to deployment of U.S. military forces for combat or peacekeeping in the Balkan region. The House adopted H.Con.Res. 42 on March 11, 1999, which authorized the President to send troops as peacekeepers; the Senate passed a non-binding resolution (S.Con.Res. 21) on March 23, 1999, that expressed the sense of Congress that the President was authorized to conduct military air operations in cooperation with NATO allies against Yugoslavia. However, the House later defeated the Senate resolution, on April 28, 1999. Other House or Senate votes sent conflicting signals in addressing funding related to troop deployments in the region, declaration of war issues, and executive and congressional roles in sending U.S. military forces abroad.

For more detailed contextual and legislative history, see CRS Report RL33532, *War Powers Resolution: Presidential Compliance*, by Richard F. Grimmett, and CRS Report RL3 1053, *Kosovo and U.S. Policy*, by Steven Woehrel and Julie Kim. The following legislation is representative of what was introduced and voted on in the 106th Congress.

Congress	Bill and Title	Description and Comments	Votes
106th	**H.Res. 103**	Provides for consideration of the concurrent resolution, H.Con.Res. 42, regarding the use of U.S. Armed Forces as part of a NATO peacekeeping operation implementing a Kosovo peace agreement. Motion to order the previous question (thus ending debate and the possibility of amendment) on adoption of H.Res. 103.	Measure agreed to in House March 11, 1999 218-201 (vote #46)
	H.Con.Res. 42 Peacekeeping Operations in Kosovo Resolution	A concurrent resolution authorizing the President to deploy U.S. Armed Forces personnel to Kosovo as part of a NATO peacekeeping operation implementing a Kosovo peace agreement, subject to certain limitations	Measure agreed to in House March 11, 1999 219-191 (vote #49)
	H.Amdt. 25 to H.Con.Res. 42	Fowler amendment to limit the deployment of U.S. Armed Forces to Kosovo and to not authorize the President to deploy ground forces as part of a NATO peacekeeping operation.	Rejected in House March 11, 1999 178-237 (vote #48)

Table. Continued

Cong-ress	Bill and Title	Description and Comments	Votes
	S. 544 Emergency Suppleme-tal Appropri-tions Act for Fiscal Year 1999	An original bill making emergency supplemental appropriations and rescissions for recovery from natural disa s t e r s, and foreign assistance, for the fiscal year ending September 30, 1999, and for other purposes. March 23, 1999: Cloture motion (thus limiting debate) on the Lott amendment (S.Amdt. 124) to the Hutchison amendment (S.Amdt. 81) to prohibit the use of funds for military operations in Yugoslavia unless Congress enacts specific authorizations in law for the conduct of those operations.	Cloture motion rejected in Senate March 23, 1999 55-44 (vote #55) Measure passed Senate March 23, 1999 (voice vote)
106th	**S.Con.Res 21**	A concurrent resolution authorizing the President of the United States to conduct military air operations and missile strikes against Yugoslavia.	Measure agreed to in Senate March 23, 1999 58-41 (vote #57) Measure rejected in House April 28, 1999 213-213 (vote #103)
	H.Res. 130	Expresses the support of the House of Representatives for the members of the U.S. Armed Forces who are engaged in military operations against Yugoslavia.	Measure agreed to in House March 24, 1999 424-1 (vote #71)
	H.R. 1141 (P.L. 106-31) 1999 Emergency Suppleme-tal **Appropria-**	A bill making emergency supplemental appropriations for the fiscal year ending September 30, 1999, and for other purposes — provides $15 billion for Central American humanitarian relief, aid to Jordan, U.S. farmer assistance, and U.S. military and humanitarian	Measure passed House March 24, 1999 220-211 (vote #70) Measure passed Senate, as amended, in lieu

	tions Act	operations in the Balkans.	of S. 544 March 24, 1999 (voice vote) House adopted conference report May 18, 1999 269-158 (vote #133) Senate adopted conference report May 20, 1999 64-36 (vote #136)
106th	**H.Res. 151**	Provides for consideration of the bill (H.R. 1569) to prohibit the use of funds appropriated to the Department of Defense from being used for the deployment of ground elements of the U.S. Armed Forces in Yugoslavia unless that deployment is specifically authorized by law; for consideration of the concurrent resolution (H.Con.Res. 82) directing the President, pursuant to Section 5(c) of the War Powers Resolution, to remove U.S. Armed Forces from their positions in connection with the present operations against Yugoslavia; for consideration of the joint resolution (H.J.Res. 44) declaring a state of war between the United States and the Government of Yugoslavia; and for consideration of the concurrent res o l u tion (S.Con.Res. 21) authorizing the President of the United States to conduct military air operations and missile strikes against Yugoslavia.	Measure agreed to in House April 28, 1999 213-210 (vote #99)

Table. Continued

Congress	Bill and Title	Description and Comments	Votes
	H.R. 1569 Military Operations in the Federal Republic of Yugoslavia Limitation Act of 1999	A bill to prohibit the use of funds appropriated to the Department of Defense from being used for the deployment of ground elements of the U.S. Armed Forces in Yugoslavia unless that deployment is specifically authorized by law.	Measure passed House April 28, 1999 249-180 (vote #100)
	H.Con.Res. 82	A concurrent resolution directing the President, pursuant to Section 5(c) of the War Powers Resolution, to remove U.S. Armed Forces from their positions in connection with the present operations against Yugoslavia.	Measure rejected in House April 28, 1999 139-290 (vote #101)
106th	**H.J.Res 44**	A joint resolution declaring a state of war between the United States and the government of Yugoslavia	Measure rejected in House April 28, 1999 2-427 (vote #102)
	S.J.Res. 20	A joint resolution authorizing the President to use all necessary force and other means, in concert with the U.S. allies, to accomplish U.S. and NATO objectives in Yugoslavia.	Motion to table agreed to in Senate May 4, 1999 78-22 (vote #98)
	H.Res. 159	Provides for consideration of the bill (H.R. 1664) making emergency supplemental	Measure agreed to in House May 6, 1999 253-171 (vote #116)

		appropriations for military operations, refugee relief, and humanitarian assistance relating to the conflict in Kosovo ... for the fiscal year ending September 30, 1999, and for other purposes.	
	H.R. 1664 (P.L. 106-51) Kosovo Emergency Supplemental Appropriations bill	A bill (as introduced) making emergency supplemental appropriations for military operations, refugee relief, and humanitarian assistance relating to the conflict in Kosovo ... for the fiscal year ending September 30, 1999, and for other purposes — provided $13.1 billion relating to Kosovo operations and other purposes (Kosovo-related supplemental funding was ultimately removed from this legislation and included in H.R. 1141).	Measure passed House as amended May 6, 1999 311-105 (vote #120)
	H.Amdt. 68 to H.R. 1664	Obey amendment to provide the President's funding request for military operations in Kosovo, etc.	Rejected in House May 6, 1999 164-260 (vote #118)
	H.Amdt. 76 to H.R. 1664	Istook amendment to prohibit funding for the implementation of any plan to invade Yugoslavia with ground forces, except in time of war.	Rejected in House May 6, 1999 117-301 (vote #119)

Table. Continued

Congress	Bill and Title	Description and Comments	Votes
106th	**S. 1059 (P.L. 106-65)** National Defense Authorization Act for Fiscal Year 2000	An original bill to authorize appropriations for FY2000 for military activities of the Department of Defense ... and for other purposes.	Measure passed Senate as amended May 27, 1999 92-3 (vote #154) Measure passed House, in lieu of H.R. 1401 June 14, 1999 (voice vote) House adopted conference report September 15, 1999 375-45 (vote #424) Senate adopted conference report September 22, 1999 (voice vote)
	S.Amdt. 383 to S. 1059	Specter amendment to direct the President, pursuant to the U.S. Constitution and the War Powers Resolution, to seek approval from Congress prior to the introduction of ground troops from the U.S. Armed Forces in connection with the present operations against Yugoslavia or funding for that operation will not be authorized.	Motion to table agreed to in Senate May 25, 1999 52-48 (vote #145)
	S.Amdt. 406 to S. 1059	B. Smith amendment to prohibit, effective October 1, 1999, the use of funds for military operations in Yugoslavia unless Congress enacts specific authorization in law for the conduct of those operations.	Motion to table agreed to in Senate May 26, 1999 77-21 (vote #151)

	H.R. 1401 National Defense Authorization Act for Fiscal Year 2000	A bill to authorize appropriations for fiscal years 2000 and 2001 for military activities of the Department of Defense ... and for other purposes.	Measure passed House June 10, 1999 365-58 (vote #191)
106th	**H.Amdt. 160 to H.R. 1401**	Souder amendment to prohibit any FY2000 funding for military operations in Yugoslavia.	Rejected in House June 10, 1999 97-328 (vote #187)
	H.Amdt. 161 to H.R. 1401	Skelton amendment to delete language which prohibits any funding for combat or peacekeeping operations in Yugoslavia after September 30, 1999; retains language which requires the President to request supplem ental appropriations in order to con d u ct com b at or peacekeeping operations in Yugoslavia.	Agreed to in House June 10, 1999 270-155 (vote #189)

TERRORIST ATTACK AGAINST AMERICA (2001)

On September 11, 2001, terrorists attacked the United States with a coordinated series of aircraft hijackings and suicide crashes into populated buildings. Two airplanes crashed into the twin towers of the World Trade Center in New York City, causing their complete destruction. Another airplane crashed into the Pentagon, and a fourth airplane crashed in southwestern Pennsylvania (near Shanksville) after passengers attempted to take control of the aircraft in order to prevent it from crashing into an important symbol of democracy and freedom, perhaps in the Washington, D.C. area. Over 3,000 people lost their lives in these terrorist attacks.

Consequently, on September 14, 2001, Congress passed a joint resolution, which "authorizes the President to use all necessary and appropriate force against those nations, organizations, or persons he determines planned, authorized, committed, or aided the terrorist attacks that occurred on September 11, 2001, or harbored such organizations or persons, in order to prevent any future acts of international terrorism against the United States by such nations, organizations, or persons." It further states that the act is intended to constitute specific statutory authorization within the meaning of the War Powers Resolution. President George W. Bush signed the joint resolution into law on September 18, 2001. On October 9, 2001, President Bush reported in a letter to Congress that U.S. Armed Forces had begun combat action in Afghanistan against the Al Qaeda terrorists and their Taliban supporters starting at 12:30 p.m. (EDT) on October 7, 2001.

Cong-ress	Bill and Title	Description and Comments	Votes
107th	**H.J.Res 64** Authorization for Use of Military Force	Joint resolution to authorize the use of United States armed forces against those responsible for the recent (September 11, 2001) attacks launched against the United States.	Measure passed House September 14, 2001 420-1 (vote #342)
	S.J.Res. 23 (P.L. 107-40)[a]	Joint resolution to authorize the use of United States armed forces against those responsible for the recent (September 11, 2001) attacks launched against the United States.	Measure passed Senate September 14, 2001 98-0 (vote #281)

[a] For a legislative history of P.L. 107-40, see CRS Report RS22357, Authorization For Use Of Military Force in Response to the 9/11 Attacks (P.L. 107-40): Lsegislative History, by Richard F. Grimmett.

USE OF FORCE AGAINST IRAQ (2002-2003)

On October 10, 2002, after several days of debate, the House passed H.J.Res. 114, which authorized the use of military force against Iraq. The Senate had considered its own measure, S.J.Res. 45, beginning on October 3, but indefinitely postponed it, and passed H.J.Res. 114 instead on October 11, 2002. As enacted into law, the joint resolution provides authorization for the use of military force against Iraq and expresses support for the President's efforts to

1. strictly enforce through the United Nations Security Council all relevant Security Council resolutions regarding Iraq; and
2. obtain prompt and decisive action by the Security Council to ensure that Iraq abandons its strategy of delay, evasion, and noncompliance and promptly and strictly complies with all relevant Security Council resolutions.

In addition, it authorizes the President to use the U.S. Armed Forces to (1) defend U.S. national security against the continuing threat posed by Iraq; and (2) enforce all relevant Security Council resolutions regarding Iraq. It directs the President, prior to or as soon as possible (but no later than 48 hours) after exercising such authority, to make available to the Speaker of the House of Representatives and the President pro tempore of the Senate his determination that

1. reliance on further diplomatic or peaceful means alone will not achieve the above purposes; and
2. acting pursuant to this joint resolution is consistent with the United States and other countries continuing to take necessary actions against international terrorists and terrorist organizations, including those who planned, authorized, committed, or aided the terrorist attacks of September 11, 2001.

It declares that this section is intended to constitute specific statutory authorization for use of the armed forces, consistent with the requirements of the War Powers Resolution. Finally, it requires the President to report to Congress at least every 60 days on matters relevant to this resolution.

The war with Iraq (Operation Iraqi Freedom) began on March 19, 2003, with an aerial attack against a location where Iraqi President Saddam Hussein was suspected to be meeting with top Iraqi officials. U.S. and British troops entered Iraq on March 20, 2003, and while the invasion encountered resistance, particularly in its early stages, U.S. forces had largely gained control of Baghdad by April 9, 2003. The northern cities of Kirkuk and Mosul fell shortly afterward, and on April 14, 2003, U.S. troops entered Tikrit, Saddam' s birthplace and the last major population center outside coalition control. On April 15, 2003, President Bush declared that "the regime of Saddam Hussein is no more."

Congress	Bill and Title	Description and Comments	Votes
107th	**H.J.Res. 114 (P.L. 107-243)**	Joint resolution to authorize the use of United States Armed Forces against Iraq.	Measure passed House October 10, 2002 296-133 (vote #455) Measure passed Senate October 11, 2002 77-23 (vote #237)
	H.Amdt. 608 to **H.J.Res. 114**	B. Lee amendment that would urge the President to work through the United Nations to ensure that Iraq is not developing weapons of mass destruction, and to urge the use of peaceful means to resolve the issue, including the resumption of weapons inspections.	Rejected in House October 10, 2002 72-355 (vote #452)
107th	**H.Amdt. 609** to **H.J.Res. 114**	Spratt amendment to authorize the U.S. military to support any new U.N. Security Council resolution that orders the elimination, by force if required, of Iraq's weapons of mass destruction, long-range missiles, and the means of producing such weapons. The President would be required to seek congressional authority before using military force against Iraq without such a	Rejected in House October 10, 2002 155-270 (vote #453)

		U.N. resolution.	
		Kucinich motion to recommit the bill to the House International Relations Committee with instructions that it be reported back with language that would require the President, prior to the use of force, to report to Congress on the effect of war with Iraq, including estimates of its impact on the U.S. economy, Iraqi citizens, and international stability.	Rejected in House October 10, 2002 101-325 (vote #454)
	S.J.Res. 45	Joint resolution to authorize the use of United States Armed Forces against Iraq.	Indefinitely postponed by Senate October 11, 2002 (unanimous consent)
		McCain motion to table the Graham amendment (S.Amdt. 4857) to the Lieberman substitute amendment (S.Amdt. 4856). The Graham amendment would authorize the use of force against Iraq and five terrorist organizations. It would require the Administration to report to Congress that diplomatic options have been exhausted no later than 48 hours after action has begun. The President would be required to report to Congress at least every 60 days.	Agreed to in Senate October 9, 2002 88-1 (vote #231)

Table. Continued

Congress	Bill and Title	Description and Comments	Votes
107th	**S.Amdt. 4869** to **S.J.Res. 45**	Byrd amendment to the Lieberman substitute amendment (S.Amdt. 4856). The Byrd amendment would provide for the termination of congressional authorization of the use of force 12 months after the resolution's enactment, unless the President certifies that an extension is necessary and Congress does not pass a joint resolution disapproving of the extension.	Rejected in Senate October 10, 2002 31-6 (vote #232)
		Motion to invoke cloture (thus limiting debate) on the Lieberman substitute amendment (S.Amdt. 4856) that would authorize the use of force against Iraqa n d require the Administration to report to Congress that diplomatic options have been exhausted no later than 48 hours after military action has begun. The President also would be required to submit a progress report to Congress at least every 60 days.	Agreed to in Senate October 10, 2002 75-25 (vote #233)
	S.Amdt. 4868 to **S.J.Res. 45**	Byrd amendment to the Lieberman substitute amendment (S.Amdt. 4856). The Byrd amendment would clarify that any authorization of the use of force against Iraq would not alter the constitutional authority of Congress to declare war. It also would clarify that no additional	Rejected in Senate October 10, 2002 14-86 (vote #234)

		authority not directly related to a clear threat of imminent, sudden, and direct attack on the United States be granted to the President unless Congress authorizes it.	
107th	**S.Amdt. 4862** to **S.J.Res. 45**	Levin amendment to the Lieberman substitute amendment (S.Amdt. 4856). The Levin amendment would authorize the use of force against Iraq if it failed to comply with a new U.N. resolution that demanded unrestricted access for U.N. weapons inspectors in Iraq and authorized the use of military force by U.N. members to enforce the resolution. Congress could return to session at any time to promptly consider proposals related to Iraq if the U.N. failed to adopt such a resolution.	Rejected in Senate October 10, 2002 24-75 (vote #235)
	S.Amdt. 4865 to **S.J.Res. 45**	Durbin amendment to the Lieberman substitute amendment (S.Amdt. 4856). The Durbin amendment would authorize the use of military force to cover an "imminent threat" by Iraq's weapons of mass destruction, rather than a "continuing threat" by Iraq.	Rejected in Senate October 10, 2002 30-70 (vote #236)
108th	**S.Res. 95**	A resolution commending the President and the armed forces of the United States of America in the conflict against Iraq.	Measure agreed to in Senate March 20, 2003 99-0 (vote #61)

Table. Continued

Congress	Bill and Title	Description and Comments	Votes
	H.Con.Res. 104	A concurrent resolution expressing the support and appreciation of the nation for the President and the members of the armed forces who are participating in Operation Iraqi Freedom.	Measure agreed to in House March 21, 2003 392-11 (vote #83)

WAR IN IRAQ AND AFGHANISTAN (2003-PRESENT)

On March 25, 2003, President Bush requested $74.8 billion in the FY2003 Emergency Supplemental for the ongoing military operations in Iraq, postwar occupation, reconstruction and relief in Iraq, and international assistance to countries contributing to the war in Iraq or the global war on terrorism. The cost of the continued U.S. presence in Afghanistan and additional funds for homeland security were also included. H.R. 1559, enacted into law as P.L. 108-11 on April 16, 2003, provided $78.49 billion in funding for these purposes. The Senate passed H.R. 1559 in lieu of its version, S. 762, by unanimous consent.

On September 17, 2003, President Bush formally requested an additional $87 billion for the ongoing military operations and for reconstruction assistance in Iraq, Afghanistan, and elsewhere. H.R. 3289 (FY2004 supplemental appropriations for Iraq, Afghanistan, and the global war on terrorism) was enacted into law as P.L. 108- 106 on November 6, 2003, providing $87.5 billion in funding. The House approved the conference agreement by a roll call vote on October 31, 2003, and the Senate approved the conference agreement by voice vote on November 3, 2003. Earlier, on October 17, 2003, the Senate had approved its own version of the measure, S. 1689, but vitiated its passage and returned the bill to the Senate Calendar.

Congress	Bill and Title	Description and Comments	Votes
108th	**H.R. 1559 (P.L. 108-11)** Emergency Wartime Supplemental Appropriations Act, 2003	A bill making emergency wartime supplemental appropriations for the fiscal year ending September 30, 2003, and for other purposes.	Measure passed House April 3, 2003 414-12 (vote #108) Measure passed Senate in lieu of S. 762 April 7, 2003 (unanimous consent) House adopted conference report April 12, 2003 (voice vote) Senate adopted conference report April 12, 2003 (unanimous consent)
	S. 762 Supplemental Appropriations Act to Support Department of Defense Operations in Iraq for Fiscal Year 2003	An original bill making supplemental appropriations to support Department of Defense operations in Iraq, Department of Homeland Security, and related efforts for the fiscal year ending September 30, 2003, and for other purposes.	Measure passed Senate April 3, 2003 93-0 (vote #125)
108th		Cochran motion to table the Hollings amendment **(S.Amdt. 479)** that would express the sense of the Senate that the President should submit a report to the Senate Finance Committee on a plan to raise revenues to offset the funds in the bill spent on the war with Iraq.	Motion agreed to in Senate April 3, 2003 79-18 (vote #121)

Table. Continued

Congress	Bill and Title	Description and Comments	Votes
	S.Amdt. 455 to S. 762	Kohl amendment to appropriate $600 million for food assistance to the people of Iraq.	Agreed to in Senate April 3, 2003 67-26 (vote #124)
	H.R. 3289 (P.L. 108-106) Emergency Supplemental Appropriations Act for Defense and for the Reconstruction of Iraq and Afghanistan, 2004	A bill making emergency supplemental appropriations for defense and for the reconstruction of Iraq and Afghanistan for the fiscal year ending September 30, 2004, and for other purposes.	Measure passed House October 17, 2003 303-125 (vote #562) Measure passed Senate with an amendment October 17, 2003 (unanimous consent) House adopted conference report October 31, 2003 298-11 (vote #601) Senate adopted conference report November 3, 2003 (voice vote)
	H.Amdt. 409 to H.R. 3289	Obey amendment to require that half of all reconstruction aid to Iraq be in the form of loans.	Rejected in House October 16, 2003 200-226 (vote #546)
108th	**H.Amdt. 407 to H.R. 3289**	Obey amendment to transfer $3.6 billion in Iraq reconstruction funds for quality of life enhancements for U.S. service members.	Rejected in House October 16, 2003 209-216 (vote #547)
	H.Amdt. 4109 to H.R. 3289	Waxman amendment to reduce Iraqi reconstruction funds in the bill by $250	Rejected in House October 16, 2003 197-224

		million.	(vote #548)
	H.Amdt. 411 to H.R. 3289	Kirk amendment to strike the provision of the bill that would allow noncompetitive contracts to be reported to Congress seven days after the contract has been awarded in certain circumstances; executive agencies would be required to inform Congress of "no-bid" contracts before they are offered.	Agreed to in House October 16, 2003 405-20 (vote #549)
	H.Amdt. 415 to H.R. 3289	Holt amendment to strike $900 million from the bill for importing petroleum products into Iraq.	Rejected in House October 16, 2003 169-256 (vote #551)
	H.Amdt. 421 to H.R. 3289	Loretta Sanchez amendment to bar the Secretary of Defense from carrying out military construction projects in excess of $1.5 million outside Iraq without prior notification to Congress.	Rejected in House October 16, 2003 128-295 (vote #552)
	H.Amdt. 422 to H.R. 3289	Kind amendment to reduce reconstruction funds for Iraq in the bill by 50%.	Rejected in House October 17, 2003 156-267, 1 Present (vote #553)
	H.Amdt. 423 to H.R. 3289	Stupak amendment to increase military pay in the bill by $265 million to cover $1,500 bonuses for each service member in Iraq and Afghanistan in FY2004.	Rejected in House October 17, 2003 213-213 (vote # 554)

Table. Continued

Congress	Bill and Title	Description and Comments	Votes
	H.Amdt. 431 to H.R. 3289	Sherman amendment to require normal competitive bidding procedures for all government contracts relating to Iraq's oil infrastructure.	Agreed to in House October 17, 2003 248-179 (vote #557)
108th	**H.R. 3289**	Obey motion to instruct House conferees to insist on provisions in the Senate bill that would structure $10 billion of the $20.3 billion in reconstruction aid to Iraq in the form of loans subject to certain conditions (and for other purposes).	Motion agreed to in House October 21, 2003 277-139 (vote #567)
	H.R. 3289	Obey motion to recommit the conference report to the conference committee with instructions that it be reported back to the House with provisions that would put half the reconstruction aid to Iraq in the form of loans (and for other purposes).	Motion rejected in the House October 31, 2003 198-221 (vote #600)
	S. 1689 Emergency Supplemental Appropriations for Iraq and Afghanistan Security and Reconstruction Act, 2004	An original bill making emergency supplemental appropriations for Iraq and Afghanistan security and reconstruction for the fiscal year ending September 30, 2004, and for other purposes.	Measure passed Senate October 17, 2003 87-12 (vote #400)
	S.Amdt. 1794 to S. 1689	Byrd amendment to eliminate $15.2 billion of the $20.3 billion allocated for Iraqi reconstruction efforts. The remaining $5.1	Rejected in Senate October 1, 2003 38-59 (vote #371)

		billion would be used for security, including pu blic safety requirement, national security, and justice purposes.	
	S.Amdt. 1795 to S. 1689	McConnell amendment that expresses the sense of the Senate thanking U.S. troops serving in Iraq and Afghanistan and extending condolences to the families of those who have been killed or injured.	Agreed to in Senate October 2, 2003 98-1 (vote #372)
108th	**S. 1689**	Stevens motion to table the Biden amendment **(S.Amdt. 1796)** that would offset Iraqi reconstruction costs by eliminating income tax cuts enacted in 2001 for the top 1% of earners.	Motion agreed to in Senate October 2, 2003 57-42 (vote #373)
		Stevens motion to table the Leahy amendment (S.Amdt. 1803) that would remove the Coalition Provisional Authority in Iraq from Defense Department control and place it under the jurisdiction of the State Department within 60 days after the bill's enactment.	Motion agreed to in Senate October 2, 2003 56-42 (vote #374)
		Stevens motion to table the Dodd amendment **(S.Amdt. 1817)** that would add $322 million to the bill's spending on battlefield clearance and safety equipment for U.S. troops in Iraq. The money would be offset by a reduction in Iraqi reconstruction funds.	Motion agreed to in Senate October 2, 2003 49-37 (vote #376)

Table. Continued

Congress	Bill and Title	Description and Comments	Votes
		Division I of the Bingaman amendment (S.Amdt. 1830) that would authorize the Defense Department to award the Iraqi Liberation Medal to any person who served in any capacity in the armed forces in Southwest Asia in connection with "Operation Iraqi Freedom."	Rejected in Senate October 14, 2003 47-48 (vote #378)
		Stevens motion to table the Stabenow amendment **(S.Amdt. 1823)** that would reduce the amount provided for Iraqi reconstruction by $5.03 billion and redirect that funding for domestic programs. Also would express the sense of the Senate that Congress should consider an additional $5.03 billion in funding for Iraqi reconstruction during the fiscal 2005 budget and appropriations process.	Motion agreed to in Senate October 14, 2003 59-35 (vote #379)
		Stevens motion to table the Dorgan amendment **(S.Amdt. 1826**) that would strike $20.3 billion in appropriatio n s f o r I r aqi reconstruction funds and require the President to direct the head of the Coalition Provisional Authority in Iraq to establish an Iraq Reconstruction Finance Authority.	Motion agreed to in Senate October 14, 2003 57-39 (vote #380)

		Stevens motion to table the Reed amendment (S.Amdt. 1834) that would authorize an additional 10,000 in Army personnel. Additional personnel would be required to be trained, incorporated into an appropriate force structure, and used for constabulary duty such as military police and light infantry. It would also require that $409 million be made available from the Iraqi Freedom Fund to fund the additional personnel.	Motion rejected in Senate October 14, 2003 45-52 (vote #382)
	S.Amdt. 1846 to S. 1689	Byrd amendment to require the Coalition Provisional Authority to report to Congress quarterly on the costs related to reconstruction activities and the revenue provided by foreign nations and international organizations. It would also require the Comptroller General to conduct an ongoing audit of the Coalition Provisional Authority to evaluate the reconstruction and security activities in Iraq.	Agreed to in Senate October 15, 2003 97-0 (vote #383)
	S.Amdt. 1806 to S. 1689	Graham amendment to express the sense of Congress that the removal of the government of Iraq under Saddam Hussein has enhanced the security of Israel and other U.S. allies.	Agreed to in Senate October 15, 2003 95-2 (vote #384)

Table. Continued

Congress	Bill and Title	Description and Comments	Votes
	S. 1689	Stevens motion to table the Byrd amendment (S.Amdt. 1818) that would appropriate $5.1 billion in security funding immediately and up to $5 billion for Iraqi reconstruction funding before April 1. The remaining $10.2 billion in reconstruction funding could be released after April 1 as part of a separate appropriations bill — but only if the United Nations had adopted a new resolution authorizing a multinational military force under U.S. leadership in Iraq, with U.N. leadership in political and economic reconstruction. The President would also be required to provide a detailed reconstruction plan that includes an estimated schedule for the transfer of sovereignty to the Iraqi people and the withdrawal of troops.	Motion agreed to in Senate October 16, 2003 57-42 (vote #385)
		Stevens motion to table the Lautenberg amendment **(S.Amdt. 1868)** that would prohibit the use of Iraqi reconstruction funds for any contact or financial agreement with an entity that pays deferred compensation to the President, Vice President, or a Cabinet-level official, or any entity in which the President,	Motion agreed to in Senate October 16, 2003 65-34 (vote #386)

		Vice President, or Cabinet-level official holds options to purchase more than 1,000 shares of stock.	
	S.Amdt. 1874 to S. 1689	McConnell amendment to express the sense of the Senate that the Secretary of Defense should issue necessary regulations to implement and begin awarding the Global War on Terrorism Medal to members of the armed forces serving in Operation Iraqi Freedom, Operation Enduring Freedom, and Operation Noble Eagle.	Agreed to in Senate October 16, 2003 97-1 (vote #387)
	S.Amdt. 1876 to S. 1689	Nickles amendment to express the sense of the Senate that all countries that hold debt from loans for the former Iraqi regime of Saddam Hussein should be urged to forgive their debt.	Agreed to in Senate October 16, 2003 98-0 (vote #388)
	S.Amdt. 1871 to S. 1689	Bayh amendment to provide a total of $10.3 billion as a grant to rebuild Iraq, including $5.1 billion for security and $5.2 billion for reconstruction costs. The remaining $10 billion would be structured as a loan to be converted to a grant if 90% of all bilateral debt incurred by the former Iraqi regime of Saddam Hussein has been forgiven by other countries (and for other related purposes).	Agreed to in Senate October 16, 2003 51-47 (vote #389)

Table. Continued

Congress	Bill and Title	Description and Comments	Votes
	S.Amdt. 1837 to S. 1689	Durbin amendment to require that a federal employee who takes leave without pay in order to perform certain service as a member of the uniformed service or the National Guard, be reimbursed for the difference between their salary and the pay and allowances they receive while on duty.	Agreed to in Senate October 17, 2003 96-3 (vote #390)
	S. 1689	Stevens motion to table the Daschle amendment (S.Amdt. 1854) that would require the President to certify that future appropriations which exceed the amount in the bill are equal to or exceeded by contributions by the international community. The requirement could be waived if the President provides a report to Congress that determines the funding is in the national security interests of the United States.	Motion agreed to in Senate October 17, 2003 55-44 (vote #391)
108th		Stevens motion to table the Landrieu amendment (S.Amdt. 1859) that would require the President to direct the head of the Coalition Provisional Authority in Iraq to establish an Iraq Reconstruction Finance Authority. The Authority would be required to obtain financing for the reconstructi o n o f Ir a q 's infrastructure through the issuance of securities and loans and by collateralizing future revenue from its oil reserves.	Motion agreed to in Senate October 17, 2003 52-47 (vote #392)
	S.Amdt.	Boxer amendment to reimburse	Agreed to in

	1843 to S. 1689	service members who paid for meals while hospitalized as a result of injuries or illness while in combat or training since September 11, 2001.	Senate October 17, 2003 99-0 (vote #393)
	S. 1689	Stevens motion to table the Corzine amendment (S.Amdt. 1882) that would establish a 12-member independe n t, b i partisan commission to examine and report on the role of policy makers in the development and use of intelligence related to Iraq and Operation Iraqi Freedom. The amendment would authorize $5 million for the commission.	Motion agreed to in Senate October 17, 2003 67-32 (vote #395)
		Stevens motion to table the Byrd amendment (S.Amdt. 1819) that would limit the use of reconstruction funds for certain programs and projects, reduce reconstruction funding by $1.65 billion, and reallocate the funds to other purposes, such as destroying conventional weapons in Iraq and accelerating reconstruction in Afghanistan.	Motion agreed to in Senate October 17, 2003 51-47 (vote #396)
		Stevens motion to table the Byrd amendment (S.Amdt. 1886) that would prohibit the use of funds in the bill for the involuntary deployment overseas for Operation Iraqi Freedom of members of the National Guard and Reserves who have been involuntarily deployed for six months or more during the past six years.	Motion agreed to in Senate October 17, 2003 82-15 (vote #397)

Table. Continued

Congress	Bill and Title	Description and Comments	Votes
		Stevens motion to table the Byrd amendment (S.Amdt. 1888) that would strike a provision in the bill that allows the President to reallocate funds for the reconstruction of Iraq and insert a provision that would require the President to seek additional funding i n subsequent appropriations bills.	Motion agreed to in Senate October 17, 2003 49-46 (vote #398)
		Stevens motion to table the Brownback amendment (S.Amdt. 1885) that would decrease the amount in the bill for Iraqi reconstruction by $600 million and increase the amount available to the Iraqi Civil Defense Corps by $50 million (and for other purposes).	Motion agreed to in Senate October 17, 2003 55-43 (vote #399)
	H.Res. 557	Commends the members of the U.S. Armed Forces and Coalition forces for liberating Iraq and expresses its gratitude for their valiant service.	Agreed to in House March 17, 2004 327-93, 7 Present (vote #64)
	H.Res. 627	Expresses deep appreciation to the members of the Armed Forces who have selflessly served, or are so serving, in Operation Iraqi Freedom.	Agreed to in House May 6, 2004 365-50 (vote #150)
	S. 2400 (P.L. 108-375) Ronald W. Reagan National Defense	Authorizes the Secretary, during FY2005 through 2009, to increase as necessary by up to 30,000 the end strength authorized for the Army to support the Army's operational mission in Iraq and	Measure passed Senate June 23, 2004 97-0 (vote #146)

	Authorization Act for Fiscal Year 2005.	Afghanistan and to achieve Army transformational reorganization objectives. Requires a fiscal year's budget to be amended to reflect any such increase. Authorizes supplemental appropriations of $25 billion for DOD for FY2005, to be available only for activities in support of operations in Iraq and Afghanistan. Allocates such funds among specified military department and defense-wide accounts. A llows such authorization only to the extent that a budget request is transmitted from the President to Congress that includes a designation of the requested amount as an emergency and essential to support activities in such countries. Provides certain transfer authority limits. Directs the Secretary to report monthly to the defense and appropriations committees on the use of such authorized funds.	
	S.Amdt. 3260 to S. 2400	Warner amendment to authorize to be appropriated for the DOD for FY2005, $25 billion, to be available only for activities in support of operations in Iraq and Afghanistan.	Agreed to in Senate June 2, 2004 95-0 (vote #106)
	S.Amdt. 3379 to S. 2400	Biden amendment to provide funds for the security and stabilization of Iraq by suspending a portion of the reduction in the highest income tax rate for individual taxpayers.	Rejected by Senate June 17, 2004 44-53 (vote #130)

Table. Continued

Congress	Bill and Title	Description and Comments	Votes
	H.Res. 691	Expresses gratitude to the U.S. armed forces for their ongoing valiant service to their country; offers continued support to the U.S. armed forces; and reaffirms that the U.S. armed forces operating in Iraq after June 30, 2004, will remain under the full authority and control of their American commanders.	Measure agreed to in House June 25, 2004 352-57 (vote #319)
	H.R. 4613 (P.L. 108-287) Department of Defense Appropriations Act, 2005.	Appropriates additional funds, to be designated for overseas contingency operations, to DOD for military personnel, operation and maintenance, and procurement (including National Guard and reserve equipment).	Measure passed House June 25, 2004 410-12 (vote #418) Measure passed Senate July 22, 2004 96-0 (vote #163)
	S.Amdt. 3502 to H.R. 4613	Byrd amendment to express the sense of the Senate that any request for funds for a fiscal year for an ongoing military operation overseas, including operations in Afghanistan and Iraq, should be included in the annual budget of the President; and that any funds provided for such a military operation should be provided in appropriations Acts for such fiscal year through appropriations to specific accounts set forth in such acts.	Agreed to in Senate June 24, 2004 89-9 (vote #147)
	H.R. 4200 (P.L. 108-375) Ronald W. Reagan	Authorizes the Secretary of Defense, during FY2005 through 2009, to increase, by up to 30,000 for the Army and 9,000 for the Marine Corps, the end	Measure passed House October

	National Defense Authorization Act for Fiscal Year 2005	strength authorized to support operational missions in Iraq and Afghanistan. Authorizes, during FY2005, the use of up to $300 million from DOD O&M funds to provide funds for the Commanders' Emergency Response Program for enabling military commanders in Iraq to respond to urgent humanitarian relief and reconstruction requirements, and for a similar program to assist the people of Afghanistan.	10, 2004 359-14 (vote #528)
109th	**H.R. 1268 (P.L. 109-13)** FY2005 Supplemental Appropriations for Iraq and Afghanistan, Tsunami Relief, and Other Activities.	Provides funds for ongoing military operations in Iraq and Afghanistan. Expresses the sense of the Senate that (1) any request for funds for a fiscal year after 2006 for an ongoing military operation overseas, including those in Afghanistan and Iraq, should be included in the annual budget of the President submitted to Congress; (2) the President should submit to Congress an amendment to the 2006 budget setting forth detailed cost estimates for such operations; and (3) any funds for such purposes should be provided in appropriations Acts through appropriations to specific accounts. Requires additional information concerning such operations, including Operations Enduring Freedom and Iraqi Freedom, to be included in reports required under both the Emergency Supplemental Appropriations Act for Defense and for the Reconstruction of Iraq and Afghanistan, 2004, and the D e partm e nt of D e f e n s e Appropriations Act, 2005.	Conference report adopted by House May 5, 2005 368-58, 1 Present (vote #161) Conference report adopted by Senate May 10, 2005 100-0 (vote #117)

Table. Continued

Congress	Bill and Title	Description and Comments	Votes
	S.Amdt. 464 to H.R. 1268	Byrd amendment that states that it is the sense of the Senate that any request for funds for a fiscal year after FY2006 for an ongoing military operation overseas, including operations in Afghanistan and Iraq, should be included in the President's annual budget.	Agreed to in the Senate April 18, 2005 61-31 (vote #96)
	H.Amdt. 214 to H.R. 1815 National Defense Authorization Act for Fiscal Year 2006	Woolsey amendment to express the sense of Congress that the President should develop a plan for the withdrawal of U.S. military forces from Iraq and submit this plan to the congressional defense committees.	Rejected in House May 25,2005 128-300 (vote #220)
	H.Res. 383	Commends U.S. and coalition forces for liberating the Iraqi people from the repressive regime of Saddam Hussein and for their ongoing efforts in support of Iraq's freedom and stability.	Measure agreed to in House July 27, 2005 426-0 (vote #438)
	S. 1042 National Defense Authorization Act for Fiscal Year 2006	Au t h orizes emergency supplemental appropriations to DOD for FY2006 for operations in Iraq, Afghanistan, and the global war on terrorism.	Measure passed Senate November 15, 2005 98-0 (vote #326)
	S.Amdt. 2518 to S. 1042	Warner amendment to clarify and recommend changes to the policy of the United States on Iraq. States that calendar year 2006 should be a period of significant transition to full Iraqi sovereignty, with Iraqi security forces taking the lead for the security of a	Agreed to in Senate November 15, 2005 79-19 (vote #323)

		free and sovereign Iraq, thereby creating the conditions for the phased redeployment of United States forces from Iraq, and that United States military forces should not stay in Iraq any longer than required.	
109th	**S.Amdt. 2519 to S. 1042**	Levin amendment to clarify and recommend changes to the policy of the United States on Iraq. States that calendar year 2006 should be a period of significant transition to full Iraqi sovereignty, with Iraqi security forces taking the lead for the security of a free and sovereign Iraq, thereby creating the conditions for the phased redeployment of United States forces from Iraq, and that United States military forces should not stay in Iraq indefinitely.	Rejected in Senate November 15, 2005 40-58 (vote #322)
	H.Res. 571	Expresses the sense of the House of Representatives that the deployment of U.S. forces in Iraq be terminated immediately.	Measure rejected in House November 18, 2005 3-403, 6 Present (vote #608)
	H.Res. 612	Expresses the commitment of the House of Representatives to achieving victory in Iraq.	Measure agreed to in House December 16, 2005 279-109, 34 Present (vote #648)

Table. Continued

Congress	Bill and Title	Description and Comments	Votes
	H.R. 2863 Department of Defense Appropriations Act, 2006	Appropriates additional funds, to be designated for contingency operations related to the global war on terrorism. Authorizes amounts for operations in Iraq and Afghanistan to be used for the purchase of heavy and light armored vehicles. Allows O&M funds appropriated in this title to be used to provide supplies, services, transportation, and other logistical support to coalition forces supporting military and stability operations in Iraq and Afghanistan.	Measure agreed to in House December 19, 2005 308-106, 2 Present (vote #669) Measure agreed to in Senate December 21, 2005 93-0 (vote #366)
109th	**H.R. 4939 (P.L. 109-234)** Emergency Supplemental Appropriations Act for Defense, the Global War on Terror, and Hurricane Recovery, 2006	Prohibits the use of funds under this title to establish permanent U.S. military bases in Iraq, or to exercise U.S. control over Iraqi oil infrastructure or resources. (Sec. 1204) Makes emergency supplemental appropriations to the Department of Defense for: military personnel; operation and maintenance; the Afghanistan Security Forces Fund; the Iraq Security Forces Fund; the Iraq Freedom Fund; the Joint Improvised Explosive Device Defeat Fund; procurement; research, development, test and evaluation. Expresses the sense	Measure passed House March 16, 2006 348-71 (vote #65) Measure passed Senate May 4, 2006 77-21 (vote #112) House adopted conference report June 13, 2006 351-67 (vote #257) Senate adopted conference report June 15, 2006 98-1 (vote #171)

		of the Senate that: (1) any request for funds for a fiscal year after 2007 for ongoing military operations in Afghanistan and Iraq should be included in the annual budget of the President submitted to Congress; (2) such request should include a detailed justification of anticipated uses of the funds; and (3) any funds provided in a fiscal year for ongoing military operations overseas should be provided in appropriations Acts through appropriations to specific accounts. (Sec. 1313)	
	H.R. 5122 (P.L. 109-364) National Defense Authorization Act for Fiscal Year 2007	Title XV authorizes estimated future emergency supplemental appropriations for the Department of Defense for FY2007 to provide funds for additional costs due to Operation Iraqi Freedom and Operation Enduring Freedom.	Measure passed House May 11, 2006 396-31 (vote #145) Measure passed Senate (with amendment) June 22, 2006 (unanimous consent) Conference report adopted by House September 29, 2006 398-23 (vote #510) Conference report adopted by Senate September 30, 2006 (unanimous consent)

Table. Continued

Congress	Bill and Title	Description and Comments	Votes
109th	**H.R. 5631 (P.L. 109-289)** Department of Defense Appropriations Act, 2007	Title IX authorizes the Secretary of Defense to use specified Operations & Maintenance funds to support U.S. military operations in Iraq and Afghanistan.	Measure passed House June 20, 2006 407-19 (vote #305) Measure passed Senate (amended) September 7, 2006 98-0 (vote #239) Conference report adopted by House September 26, 2006 394-22 (vote #486) Conference report adopted by Senate September 29, 2006 100-0 (vote #261)
	H.Res. 861	Declares that it is not in the national security interest of the United States to set an arbitrary dat e f o r withdrawal or redeployment of United States Armed Forces from Iraq.	Measure agreed to in House June 16, 2006 256-153 (vote #288)
	S.Amdt. 4320 to S. 2766 National Defense Authorization Act for Fiscal Year 2007	Levin amendment expressing the sense of Congress that the President should begin phased redeployment of United States forces from Iraq in 2006.	Rejected in Senate June 22, 2006 39-60 (vote #182)
	S.Amdt. 4442 to S. 2766 National Defense Au thorization Act	Kerry amendment to require the redeployment of United States Armed Forces from Iraq by July 1, 2007.	Rejected in Senate June 22, 2006 13-86 (vote #181)

	for Fiscal Year 2007		
110th	**H.R. 1** Implementing the 9/11 Commission Recommendations Act of 2007	(Sec. 1441) Declares that it shall be the policy of the United States to vigorously support the government of Afghanistan by providing increased assistance and the continued deployment of United States troops as long as the Afghan government supports such United States involvement.	Measure agreed to in House January 9, 2007 299-128 (vote #15)
	S.Con.Res. 2	Expresses the sense of Congress that it is not in the U.S. national interest to deepen its military involvement in Iraq, particularly by increasing the U.S. military presence in Iraq.	Failure to invoke cloture in Senate February 1, 2007 0-97 (vote #43)
	S. 470	Expresses the sense of Congress that the Senate disagrees with the plan to augment our forces in Iraq by 21,500 and that Congress should not take any action that will endanger U.S. military forces in the field.	Failure to invoke cloture in Senate February 5, 2007 49-47 (vote #44)
	H.Con.Res. 63	Disapproving of the decision of the President announced on January 10, 2007, to deploy more than 20,000 additional United States combat troop to Iraq.	Measure agreed to in House February 16, 2007 246-182 (vote #99)

Table. Continued

Congress	Bill and Title	Description and Comments	Votes
	S. 574	Expresses the sense of Congress that Congress and the American people will continue to support and protect U.S. Armed Forces members who are serving in Iraq; and that Congress disapproves of President Bush's decision announced on January 10, 2007, to deploy more than 20,000 additional U.S. combat troops to Iraq.	Failure to invoke cloture in Senate February 17, 2007 56-34 (vote #51)
	S.J.Res. 9	Directs the President to begin the phased redeployment of U.S. forces from Iraq within 120 days of enactment of this joint resolution with the goal of redeploying by March 31, 2008, all U.S. combat forces from Iraq.	Measure rejected in Senate March 15, 2007 48-50 (vote #75)
110th	**S.Res. 107**	Declares that the President and Congress should not take any action that will endanger U.S. Armed Forces; and will provide necessary funds for training, equipment, and other support for troops in the field.	Measure agreed to in Senate March 15, 2007 96-2 (vote #76)
	S.Con.Res. 20	Expresses the sense of Congress that Congress should not take any action that will endanger U.S. military forces in the field, including the elimination or reduction of funds for troops in the field.	Agreed to in Senate March 15, 2007 82-16 (vote #77)
	H.R. 1591 U.S. Troop Readiness, Veterans' Care, Katrina Recovery, and Iraq Accountability Appropriations Act, 2007	Makes emergency supplemental appropriations for the Department of Defense for FY2007 for contingency operations directly related to the global war on terror. Prohibits any funds from being obligated or expended by the U.S. government to establish any military installation or base for the permanent stationing of U.S. Armed Forces in Iraq. Prohibits funds from	Measure passed House March 23, 2007 218-212, 1 present (vote #186) Measure passed Senate March 29, 2007 51-47

		being used to deploy any unit of the Armed Forces to Iraq unless the chief of the military department concerned has certified that such unit is fully mission capable.	(vote #126) Conference report adopted by House April 25, 2007 218-208, 2 present (vote #265) Conference report
		Prohibits funds from being used to initiate, execute, or continue any order that has the effect of extending the deployment for Operation Iraqi Freedom of any unit of the Army, Army Reserve, or Army National Guard beyond 365 days; or Marine Corps or Marine Corps Reserve beyond 210 days. Outlines specified determinations, relating to actions of the government of Iraq, that must be made by the President to Congress on or before July 1, 2007. Requires that, if the President fails to make any of the determinations, the Secretary of Defense shall commence the redeployment of U.S. Armed Forces from Iraq no later than such date, with a goal of completing such redeployment within 180 days. Requires that, if the President makes all such determinations, the Secretary shall commence such redeployment no later than October 1, 2007, with a goal of completing that redeployment within 180 days. Makes funds immediately available to plan and execute a safe and orderly redeployment.	adopted by Senate April 26, 2007 51-46 (vote #147) House failed to override veto May 2, 2007 222-203, 1 present (vote #276)

Table. Continued

Congress	Bill and Title	Description and Comments	Votes
	S.Amdt. 643 to H.R. 1591	To strike language that would tie t h e hand s o f t h e Commander-in-Chief by imposing an arbitrary timetable for the withdrawal of U.S. forces from Iraq.	Rejected in Senate March 27, 2007 48-50 (vote #116)
	H.R. 2237	Requires the Secretary of Defense to commence the redeployment of U.S. forces deployed in Iraq and prohibits any funds from being used to further deploy U.S. forces to Iraq after completion of the redeployment.	Measure failed of passage in House May 10, 2007 171-255 (vote #330)
	H.R. 2206 (P.L. 110-28) U.S. Troop Readiness, Veterans' Care, Katrina Recovery, and Iraq Accountability Appropriations Act, 2007	Makes emergency supplemental appropriations for the Department of Defense for FY2007. Requires the President to direct the orderly redeployment of U.S. forces from Iraq if the components of the Iraqi government reach a consensus directing a redeployment of U.S. Forces. Prohibits any funds from being obligated or expended by the U.S. government to establish any military installation or base for the permanent stationing of U.S. Armed Forces in Iraq.	Measure passed House May 10, 2007 221-205 (vote #333) Measure passed Senate by voice vote 5/17/2007
110th	**S.Amdt. 1098 to S.Amdt. 1097, H.R. 1495** Water Resources Development Act of 2007	The President shall commence the ... redeployment of United States forces from Iraq ... not later than 120 days after the date of the enactment of this Act. No funds ... may be obligated or expended to continue the deployment in Iraq of members of the United States Armed Forces after March 31, 2008.	Failure to invoke cloture in Senate May 16, 2007 29-67 (vote #167)

	H.R. 1585 National Defense Authorization Act for Fiscal Year 2008	Amends the Warner Act to make permanent the prohibition on the establishment of permanent military installations in Iraq. Authorizes appropriations for DOD for FY2008 to provide additional funds for Operations Iraqi Freedom and Enduring Freedom.	Measure passed House May 17, 2007 397-27 (vote #373)
	S.Amdt. 2012 to H.R. 1585	To specify minimum periods between deployment of units and members of the Armed Forces for Operation Iraqi Freedom and Operation Enduring Freedom.	Failure to invoke cloture in Senate July 11, 2007 56-41 (vote #241)
	S.Amdt. 2032 to H.R. 1585	To limit the length of deployment of members of the Armed Forced for Operation Iraqi Freedom.	Rejected in Senate July 11, 2007 52-45 (vote #243)
	S.Amdt. 2078 to H.R. 1585	To express the sense of Congress that the dwell time between extended operational deployments of members of the Armed Forces should be no less than 12 months for regular forces and no less than 5 years for reserve forces.	Rejected in Senate July 11, 2007 41-55 (vote #244)
	S.Amdt. 2087 to H.R. 1585	The Secretary of Defense shall commence the reduction of the number of United States forces in Iraq not later than 120 days after the date of the enactment of this Act ... and shall complete the transition of United States forces to a limited presence and missions ... by April 30, 2008.	Failure to invoke cloture in Senate July 18, 2007 52-47 (vote #252)

Table. Continued

Congress	Bill and Title	Description and Comments	Votes
110th	**H.R. 2956**	Directs the Secretary of Defense to commence the reduction of the number of Armed Forces in Iraq beginning no later than 120 days after the enactment of this Act and complete the reduction and transition to a limited presence in Iraq by no later than April 1, 2008.	Measure passed House July 12, 2007 223-201 (vote #624)
	H.R. 2929	Declares that it is the policy of the United States not to establish any military installation or base providing for the permanent stationing of U.S. armed forces in Iraq.	Measure passed House July 25, 2007 399-24 (vote #717)
	H.R. 3159	Prohibits any unit of the regular Armed Forces from being deployed for Operation Iraqi Freedom unless the period between the most recent previous deployment and a subsequent deployment is equal to or longer than the period of the most recent previous deployment. Expresses the sense of Congress that the optimal minimum period between such deployments should be equal to or longer than twice the period of the most recent previous deployment.	Measure passed House August 2, 2007 229-194, 3 present (vote #796)
	H.R. 3222 Department of Defense Appropriations Act, 2008	(Sec. 8103) None of the funds appropriated or otherwise made available by this or any other Act shall be obligated or expended by the United States Government ... to establish any military installation or base for the purpose of providing for the permanent stationing of	Measure passed House August 5, 2007 395-13 (vote #846)

		United States Armed Forces in Iraq. (Sec. 8106) Any request for funds for a fiscal year after fiscal year 2008 for an ongoing military operation overseas, including operations in Afghanistan and Iraq, shall be included in the annual budget of the President for such fiscal year as submitted to Congress ...	

SOURCES CONSULTED

Congressional Quarterly at [http://www.cq.com].

Legislative Information System (LIS) of the U.S. Congress at [http://www.congress.gov/].

Congressional Quarterly Almanac. Washington, CQ Press. Annual. *CQ Weekly*. Washington, CQ Press. Various issues.

CRS Report RL33532. *War Powers Resolution: Presidential Compliance*, by Richard F. Grimmett.

CRS Report RL32170.* *Instances of Use of United States Armed Forces Abroad, 1798-2004*, by Richard F. Grimmett.

CRS Report RL3 2267. *The War Powers Resolution: After Thirty Years*, by Richard F. Grimmett.

CRS Report RL31829.* *Supplemental Appropriations FY2003: Iraq Conflict, Afghanistan, Global War on Terrorism, and Homeland Security*, by Amy Belasco and Larry Nowels.

CRS Report RL32090.* *FY2004 Supplemental Appropriations for Iraq, Afghanistan, and the Global War on Terrorism: Military Operations and Reconstruction Assistance*, by Stephen Daggett, Larry Nowels, Curt Tarnoff, and Rhoda Margesson.

CRS Report RL32783.* *FY2005 Supplemental Appropriations for Iraq and Afghanistan, Tsunami Relief, and Other Activities*, by Amy Belasco and Larry Nowels.

* This CRS report has been archived and is no longer current. For copies of this report for historical perspective and background information only, please contact CRS.

In: U.S. Armed Forces Abroad 1798-2007 ISBN 978-1-60692-722-9
Editor: Richard R. Grimmett, pp. 77-126

Chapter 2

INSTANCES OF USE OF UNITED STATES ARMED FORCES ABROAD, 1798-2007*

Richard F. Grimmett

SUMMARY

This article lists hundreds of instances in which the United States has used its armed forces abroad in situations of military conflict or potential conflict or for other than normal peacetime purposes. It was compiled in part from various older lists and is intended primarily to provide a rough survey of past U.S. military ventures abroad, without reference to the magnitude of the given instance noted. The listing often contains references, especially from 1980 forward, to continuing military deployments especially U.S. military participation in multinational operations associated with NATO or the United Nations. Most of these post-1980 instances are summaries based on Presidential reports to Congress related to the War Powers Resolution. A comprehensive commentary regarding any of the instances listed is not undertaken here.

The instances differ greatly in number of forces, purpose, extent of hostilities, and legal authorization. Eleven times in its history the U.S. has formally declared war against foreign nations. These eleven U.S. war declarations encompassed five separate wars: the war with Great Britain declared in 1812, the war with Mexico

* This is an edited, excerpted and augmented edition of a CRS Report for Congress publication, Order Code RL32170, dated January 14, 2008.

declared in 1846, the War with Spain declared in 1898, the First World War, during which the U.S. declared war with Germany and with Austria-Hungary during 1917, World War II, during which the U.S. declared war against Japan, Germany, and Italy in 1941, and against Bulgaria, Hungary, and Rumania in 1942. Some of the instances were extended military engagements that might be considered undeclared wars. These include the Undeclared Naval War with France from 1798 to 1800; the First Barbary War from 1801 to 1805; the Second Barbary War of 1815; the Korean War of 1950-53; the Vietnam War from 1964 to 1973; the Persian Gulf War of 1991, global actions against foreign terrorists after the September 11, 2001 attacks on the United States, and the War with Iraq in 2003. With the exception of the Korean War, all of these conflicts received Congressional authorization in some form short of a formal declaration of war. Other, more recent instances often involve deployment of U.S. military forces as part of a multinational operation associated with NATO or the United Nations.

The majority of the instances listed prior to World War II were brief Marine or Navy actions to protect U.S. citizens or promote U.S. interests. A number were actions against pirates or bandits. Covert actions, disaster relief, and routine alliance stationing and training exercises are not included here, nor are the Civil and Revolutionary Wars and the continual use of U.S. military units in the exploration, settlement, and pacification of the Western part of the United States.

INTRODUCTION

The following list reviews hundreds of instances in which the United States has utilized military forces abroad in situations of military conflict or potential conflict to protect U.S. citizens or promote U.S. interests. The list does not include covert actions or numerous instances in which U.S. forces have been stationed abroad since World War II in occupation forces or for participation in mutual security organizations, base agreements, or routine military assistance or training operations. Because of differing judgments over the actions to be included, other lists may include more or fewer instances.[1]

[1] Other lists include Goldwater, Senator Barry. War Without Declaration. A Chronological List of 199 U.S. Military Hostilities Abroad Without a Declaration of War. 1798-1972. Congressional Record, V. 119, July 20, 1973: S 14174-14183; U.S. Department of State. Armed Actions Taken by the United States Without a Declaration of War, 1789-1967. Research Project 806A. Historical Studies Division. Bureau of Public Affairs; Collins, John M. America's Small Wars. New York, Brassey' s, 1990. For a discussion of the evolution of lists of military actions and legal authorization for various actions, see Wormuth, Francis D. and Edwin B. Firmage, To Chain the

The instances vary greatly in size of operation, legal authorization, and significance. The number of troops involved range from a few sailors or Marines landed to protect American lives and property to hundreds of thousands in Korea and Vietnam and millions in World War II. Some actions were of short duration and some lasted a number of years. In some instances a military officer acted without authorization; some actions were conducted solely under the President's powers as Chief Executive or Commander in Chief; other instances were authorized by Congress in some fashion. In eleven separate cases (listed in boldface type) the United States formally declared war against foreign nations. For most of the instances listed, however, the status of the action under domestic or international law has not been addressed. Most instances listed since 1980, are summaries of U.S. military deployments reported to Congress by the President as a result of the War Powers Resolution. Several of these Presidential reports are summaries of activities related to an on-going operation previously reported. It is important to note that inclusion in this list does not connote either legality or level of significance of the instance described. This report covers uses of U.S. military force abroad from 1798 through mid-September 2007. It will be revised as circumstances warrant.

Listing of Notable Deployments of U.S. Military Forces Overseas, 1798-2007

1798-1800 *Undeclared Naval War with France.* This contest included land actions, such as that in the Dominican Republic, city of Puerto Plata, where marines captured a French privateer under the guns of the forts. Congress authorized military action through a series of statutes.

1801-05 *Tripoli.* The First Barbary War included the U.S.S. *George Washington* and *Philadelphia* affairs and the Eaton expedition, during which a few marines landed with United States Agent William Eaton to raise a force against Tripoli in an effort to free the crew of the *Philadelphia.* Tripoli declared war but not the United States, although Congress authorized U.S. military action by statute.

Dog of War; the War Power of Congress in History and Law. Dallas, Southern Methodist University Press, 1986. p. 133-149.

1806 *Mexico (Spanish territory).* Capt. Z. M. Pike, with a platoon of troops, invaded Spanish territory at the headwaters of the Rio Grande on orders from Gen. James Wilkinson. He was made prisoner without resistance at a fort he constructed in present day Colorado, taken to Mexico, and later released after seizure of his papers.

1806-10 *Gulf of Mexico.* American gunboats operated from New Orleans against Spanish and French privateers off the Mississippi Delta, chiefly under Capt. John Shaw and Master Commandant David Porter.

1810 *West Florida (Spanish territory).* Gov. Claiborne of Louisiana, on orders of the President, occupied with troops territory in dispute east of the Mississippi River as far as the Pearl River, later the eastern boundary of Louisiana. He was authorized to seize as far east as the Perdido River.

1812 *Amelia Island and other parts of east Florida, then under Spain.* Temporary possession was authorized by President Madison and by Congress, to prevent occupation by any other power; but possession was obtained by Gen. George Matthews in so irregular a manner that his measures were disavowed by the President.

1812-15 *War of 1812. On June 18, 1812, the United States declared war between the United States and the United Kingdom of Great Britain and Ireland.* Among the issues leading to the war were British interception of neutral ships and blockades of the United States during British hostilities with France.

1813 *West Florida (Spanish territory).* On authority given by Congress, General Wilkinson seized Mobile Bay in April with 600 soldiers. A small Spanish garrison gave way. The U.S. advanced into disputed territory to the Perdido River, as projected in 1810. No fighting.

1813-14 *Marquesas Islands.* U.S. forces built a fort on the island of Nukahiva to protect three prize ships which had been captured from the British.

1814 *Spanish Florida.* Gen. Andrew Jackson took Pensacola and drove out the British with whom the United States was at war.

18 14-25 *Caribbean.* Engagements between pirates and American ships or squadrons took place repeatedly especially ashore and offshore about Cuba, Puerto Rico, Santo Domingo, and Yucatan. Three

thousand pirate attacks on merchantmen were reported between 1815 and 1823. In 1822 Commodore James Biddle employed a squadron of two frigates, four sloops of war, two brigs, four schooners, and two gunboats in the West Indies.

1815 *Algiers.* The second Barbary War was declared against the United States by the Dey of Algiers of the Barbary states, an act not reciprocated by the United States. Congress did authorize a military expedition by statutes. A large fleet under Decatur attacked Algiers and obtained indemnities.

1815 *Tripoli.* After securing an agreement from Algiers, Decatur demonstrated with his squadron at Tunis and Tripoli, where he secured indemnities for offenses during the War of 1812.

1816 *Spanish Florida.* United States forces destroyed Nicholls Fort, called also Negro Fort, which harbored raiders making forays into United States territory.

18 16-18 *Spanish Florida - First Seminole War.* The Seminole Indians, whose area was a haven for escaped slaves and border ruffians, were attacked by troops under Generals Jackson and Gaines and pursued into northern Florida. Spanish posts were attacked and occupied, British citizens executed. In 1819 the Floridas were ceded to the United States.

1817 *Amelia Island (Spanish territory off Florida).* Under orders of President Monroe, United States forces landed and expelled a group of smugglers, adventurers, and freebooters.

1818 *Oregon.* The U.S.S. *Ontario*, dispatched from Washington, landed at the Columbia River and in August took possession of Oregon territory. Britain had conceded sovereignty but Russia and Spain asserted claims to the area.

1820-23 *Africa.* Naval units raided the slave traffic pursuant to the 1819 act of Congress.

1822 *Cuba.* United States naval forces suppressing piracy landed on the northwest coast of Cuba and burned a pirate station.

1823 *Cuba.* Brief landings in pursuit of pirates occurred April 8 near Escondido; April 16 near Cayo Blanco; July 11 at Siquapa Bay; July 21 at Cape Cruz; and October 23 at Camrioca.

1824 *Cuba.* In October the U.S.S. *Porpoise* landed bluejackets near Matanzas in pursuit of pirates. This was during the cruise authorized in 1822.

1824 *Puerto Rico (Spanish territory).* Commodore David Porter with a landing party attacked the town of Fajardo which had sheltered pirates and insulted American naval officers. He landed with 200 men in November and forced an apology. Commodore Porter was later court-martialed for overstepping his powers.

1825 *Cuba.* In March cooperating American and British forces landed at Sagua La Grande to capture pirates.

1827 *Greece.* In October and November landing parties hunted pirates on the islands of Argenteire, Miconi, and Androse.

183 1-32 *Falkland Islands.* Captain Duncan of the *U.S.S. Lexington* investigated the capture of three American sealing vessels and sought to protect American interests.

1832 *Sumatra.* February 6 to 9. A naval force landed and stormed a fort to punish natives of the town of Quallah Battoo for plundering the American ship *Friendship.*

1833 *Argentina.* October 31 to November 15. A force was sent ashore at Buenos Aires to protect the interests of the United States and other countries during an insurrection.

1835-36 *Peru.* December 10, 1835, to January 24, 1836, and August 31 to December 7, 1836. Marines protected American interests in Callao and Lima during an attempted revolution.

1836 *Mexico.* General Gaines occupied Nacogdoches (Tex.), disputed territory, from July to December during the Texan war for independence, under orders to cross the "imaginary boundary line" if an Indian outbreak threatened.

1838-39 *Sumatra.* December 24, 1838, to January 4, 1839. A naval force landed to punish natives of the towns of Quallah Battoo and Muckie (Mukki) for depredations on American shipping.

1840 *Fiji Islands.* July. Naval forces landed to punish natives for attacking American exploring and surveying parties.

1841 *Drummond Island, Kingsmill Group.* A naval party landed to avenge the murder of a seaman by the natives.

1841 *Samoa.* February 24. A naval party landed and burned towns after the murder of an American seaman on Upolu Island.

1842 *Mexico.* Commodore T.A.C. Jones, in command of a squadron long cruising off California, occupied Monterey, Calif., on October 19, believing war had come. He discovered peace, withdrew, and saluted. A similar incident occurred a week later at San Diego.

1843	*China.* Sailors and marines from the *St. Louis* were landed after a clash between Americans and Chinese at the trading post in Canton.
1843	*Africa.* November 29 to December 16. Four United States vessels demonstrated and landed various parties (one of 200 marines and sailors) to discourage piracy and the slave trade along the Ivory coast, and to punish attacks by the natives on American seamen and shipping.
1844	*Mexico.* President Tyler deployed U.S. forces to protect Texas against Mexico, pending Senate approval of a treaty of annexation. (Later rejected.) He defended his action against a Senate resolution of inquiry.
1846-48	*Mexican War. On May 13, 1846, the United States recognized the existence of a state of war with Mexico.* After the annexation of Texas in 1845, the United States and Mexico failed to resolve a boundary dispute and President Polk said that it was necessary to deploy forces in Mexico to meet a threatened invasion.
1849	*Smyrna.* In July a naval force gained release of an American seized by Austrian officials.
1851	*Turkey.* After a massacre of foreigners (including Americans) at Jaffa in January, a demonstration by the Mediterranean Squadron was ordered along the Turkish (Levant) coast.
1851	*Johanns Island (east of Africa).* August. Forces from the U.S. sloop of war *Dale* exacted redress for the unlawful imprisonment of the captain of an American whaling brig.
1852-53	*Argentina.* February 3 to 12, 1852; September 17, 1852 to April 1853. Marines were landed and maintained in Buenos Aires to protect American interests during a revolution.
1853	*Nicaragua.* March 11 to 13. U.S. forces landed to protect American lives and interests during political disturbances.
1853-54	*Japan.* Commodore Perry and his naval expedition made a display of force leading to the "opening of Japan."
1853-54	*Ryukyu and Bonin Islands.* Commodore Perry on three visits before going to Japan and while waiting for a reply from Japan made a naval demonstration, landing marines twice, and secured a coaling concession from the ruler of Naha on Okinawa; he also demonstrated in the Bonin Islands with the purpose of securing facilities for commerce.

1854 *China.* April 4 to June 15 to 17. American and English ships landed forces to protect American interests in and near Shanghai during Chinese civil strife.

1854 *Nicaragua.* July 9 to 15. Naval forces bombarded and burned San Juan del Norte (Greytown) to avenge an insult to the American Minister to Nicaragua.

1855 *China.* May 19 to 21. U.S. forces protected American interests in Shanghai and, from August 3 to 5 fought pirates near Hong Kong.

1855 *Fiji Islands.* September 12 to November 4. An American naval force landed to seek reparations for depredations on American residents and seamen.

1855 *Uruguay.* November 25 to 29. United States and European naval forces landed to protect American interests during an attempted revolution in Montevideo.

1856 *Panama, Republic of New Grenada.* September 19 to 22. U.S. forces landed to protect American interests during an insurrection.

1856 *China.* October 22 to December 6. U.S. forces landed to protect American interests at Canton during hostilities between the British and the Chinese, and to avenge an assault upon an unarmed boat displaying the United States flag.

1857 *Nicaragua.* April to May, November to December. In May Commander C.H. Davis of the United States Navy, with some marines, received the surrender of William Walker, who had been attempting to get control of the country, and protected his men from the retaliation of native allies who had been fighting Walker. In November and December of the same year United States vessels *Saratoga*, *Wabash*, and *Fulton* opposed another attempt of William Walker on Nicaragua. Commodore Hiram Paulding' s act of landing marines and compelling the removal of Walker to the United States, was tacitly disavowed by Secretary of State Lewis Cass, and Paulding was forced into retirement.

1858 *Uruguay.* January 2 to 27. Forces from two United States warships landed to protect American property during a revolution in Montevideo.

1858 *Fiji Islands.* October 6 to 16. A marine expedition chastised natives for the murder of two American citizens at Waya.

1858-59 *Turkey.* The Secretary of State requested a display of naval force along the Levant after a massacre of Americans at Jaffa and mistreatment elsewhere "to remind the authorities (of Turkey) of the power of the United States."

1859 *Paraguay.* Congress authorized a naval squadron to seek redress for an attack on a naval vessel in the Parana River during 1855. Apologies were made after a large display of force.

1859 *Mexico.* Two hundred United States soldiers crossed the Rio Grande in pursuit of the Mexican bandit Cortina.

1859 *China.* July 31 to August 2. A naval force landed to protect American interests in Shanghai.

1860 *Angola, Portuguese West Africa.* March 1. American residents at Kissembo called upon American and British ships to protect lives and property during problems with natives.

1860 *Colombia(Bay of Panama).* September 27 to October 8. Naval forces landed to protect American interests during a revolution.

1863 *Japan.* July 16. The *U.S.S. Wyoming* retaliated against a firing on the American vessel *Pembroke* at Shimonoseki.

1864 *Japan.* July 14 to August 3. Naval forces protected the United States Minister to Japan when he visited Yedo to negotiate concerning some American claims against Japan, and to make his negotiations easier by impressing the Japanese with American power.

1864 *Japan.* September 4 to 14. Naval forces of the United States, Great Britain, France, and the Netherlands compelled Japan and the Prince of Nagato in particular to permit the Straits of Shimonoseki to be used by foreign shipping in accordance with treaties already signed.

1865 *Panama.* March 9 and 10. U.S. forces protected the lives and property of American residents during a revolution.

1866 *China.* From June 20 to July 7, U.S. forces punished an assault on the American consul at Newchwang.

1866 *Mexico.* To protect American residents, General Sedgwick and 100 men in November obtained surrender of Matamoras. After three days he was ordered by U.S. Government to withdraw. His act was repudiated by the President.

1867 *Nicaragua.* Marines occupied Managua and Leon.

1867 *Formosa.* June 13. A naval force landed and burned a number of huts to punish the murder of the crew of a wrecked American vessel.

1868 *Japan (Osaka, Hiolo, Nagasaki, Yokohama, and Negata).* February 4 to 8, April 4 to May 12, June 12 and 13. U.S. forces were landed to protect American interests during the civil war in Japan.

1868 *Uruguay.* February 7 and 8, 19 to 26. U.S. forces protected foreign residents and the customhouse during an insurrection at Montevideo.

1868 *Colombia.* April. U.S. forces protected passengers and treasure in transit at Aspinwall during the absence of local police or troops on the occasion of the death of the President of Colombia.

1870 *Mexico.* June 17 and 18. U.S. forces destroyed the pirate ship *Forward*, which had been run aground about 40 miles up the Rio Tecapan.

1870 *Hawaiian Islands.* September 21. U.S. forces placed the American flag at half mast upon the death of Queen Kalama, when the American consul at Honolulu would not assume responsibility for so doing.

1871 *Korea.* June 10 to 12. A U.S. naval force attacked and captured five forts to punish natives for depredations on Americans, particularly for murdering the crew of the *General Sherman* and burning the schooner, and for later firing on other American small boats taking soundings up the Salee River.

1873 *Colombia (Bay of Panama).* May 7 to 22, September 23 to October 9. U.S. forces protected American interests during hostilities between local groups over control of the government of the State of Panama.

1873-96 *Mexico.* United States troops crossed the Mexican border repeatedly in pursuit of cattle thieves and other brigands. There were some reciprocal pursuits by Mexican troops into border territory. Mexico protested frequently. Notable cases were at Remolina in May 1873 and at Las Cuevas in 1875. Washington orders often supported these excursions. Agreements between Mexico and the United States, the first in 1882, finally legitimized such raids. They continued intermittently, with minor disputes, until 1896.

1874 *Hawaiian Islands.* February 12 to 20. Detachments from American vessels were landed to preserve order and protect American lives and interests during the coronation of a new king.

1876 *Mexico.* May 18. An American force was landed to police the town of Matamoras temporarily while it was without other government.

1882 *Egypt.* July 14 to 18. American forces landed to protect American interests during warfare between British and Egyptians and looting of the city of Alexandria by Arabs.

1885 *Panama (Colon).* January 18 and 19. U.S. forces were used to guard the valuables in transit over the Panama Railroad, and the safes and vaults of the company during revolutionary activity. In March, April, and May in the cities of Colon and Panama, the forces helped reestablish freedom of transit during revolutionary activity.

1888 *Korea.* June. A naval force was sent ashore to protect American residents in Seoul during unsettled political conditions, when an outbreak of the populace was expected.

1888 *Haiti.* December 20. A display of force persuaded the Haitian Government to give up an American steamer which had been seized on the charge of breach of blockade.

1888-89 *Samoa.* November 14, 1888, to March 20, 1889. U.S. forces were landed to protect American citizens and the consulate during a native civil war.

1889 *Hawaiian Islands.* July 30 and 31. U.S. forces protected American interests at Honolulu during a revolution.

1890 *Argentina.* A naval party landed to protect U.S. consulate and legation in Buenos Aires.

1891 *Haiti.* U.S. forces sought to protect American lives and property on Navassa Island.

1891 *Bering Strait.* July 2 to October 5. Naval forces sought to stop seal poaching.

1891 *Chile.* August 28 to 30. U.S. forces protected the American consulate and the women and children who had taken refuge in it during a revolution in Valparaiso.

1893 *Hawaii.* January 16 to April 1. Marines were landed ostensibly to protect American lives and property, but many believed actually to promote a provisional government under Sanford B. Dole. This action was disavowed by the United States.

1894 *Brazil*. January. A display of naval force sought to protect American commerce and shipping at Rio de Janeiro during a Brazilian civil war.

1894 *Nicaragua*. July 6 to August 7. U.S. forces sought to protect American interests at Bluefields following a revolution.

1894-95 *China*. Marines were stationed at Tientsin and penetrated to Peking for protection purposes during the Sino-Japanese War.

1894-95 *China*. A naval vessel was beached and used as a fort at Newchwang for protection of American nationals.

1894-96 *Korea*. July 24, 1894 to April 3, 1896. A guard of marines was sent to protect the American legation and American lives and interests at Seoul during and following the Sino-Japanese War.

1895 *Colombia*. March 8 to 9. U.S. forces protected American interests during an attack on the town of Bocas del Toro by a bandit chieftain.

1896 *Nicaragua*. May 2 to 4. U.S. forces protected American interests in Corinto during political unrest.

1898 *Nicaragua*. February 7 and 8. U.S. forces protected American lives and property at San Juan del Sur.

1898 *The Spanish-American War. On April 25, 1898, the United States declared war with Spain.* The war followed a Cuban insurrection against Spanish rule and the sinking of the *U.S.S. Maine* in the harbor at Havana.

1898-99 *China*. November 5, 1898 to March 15, 1899. U.S. forces provided a guard for the legation at Peking and the consulate at Tientsin during contest between the Dowager Empress and her son.

1899 *Nicaragua*. American and British naval forces were landed to protect national interests at San Juan del Norte, February 22 to March 5, and at Bluefields a few weeks later in connection with the insurrection of Gen. Juan P. Reyes.

1899 *Samoa*. February-May 15. American and British naval forces were landed to protect national interests and to take part in a bloody contention over the succession to the throne.

1899-1901 *Philippine Islands*. U.S. forces protected American interests following the war with Spain and conquered the islands by defeating the Filipinos in their war for independence.

1900 *China*. May 24 to September 28. American troops participated in operations to protect foreign lives during the Boxer rising, particularly at Peking. For many years after this experience a permanent legation guard was maintained in Peking, and was strengthened at times as trouble threatened.

1901 *Colombia (State of Panama).* November 20 to December 4. U.S. forces protected American property on the Isthmus and kept transit lines open during serious revolutionary disturbances.

1902 *Colombia* - April 16 to 23. U.S. forces protected American lives and property at Bocas del Toro during a civil war.

1902 *Colombia (State of Panama).* September 17 to November 18. The United States placed armed guards on all trains crossing the Isthmus to keep the railroad line open, and stationed ships on both sides of Panama to prevent the landing of Colombian troops.

1903 *Honduras.* March 23 to 30 or 31. U.S. forces protected the American consulate and the steamship wharf at Puerto Cortez during a period of revolutionary activity.

1903 *Dominican Republic.* March 30 to April 21. A detachment of marines was landed to protect American interests in the city of Santo Domingo during a revolutionary outbreak.

1903 *Syria.* September 7 to 12. U.S. forces protected the American consulate in Beirut when a local Moslem uprising was feared.

1903-04 *Abyssinia.* Twenty-five marines were sent to Abyssinia to protect the U.S. Consul General while he negotiated a treaty.

1903-14 *Panama.* U.S. forces sought to protect American interests and lives during and following the revolution for independence from Colombia over construction of the Isthmian Canal. With brief intermissions, United States Marines were stationed on the Isthmus from November 4, 1903, to January 21, 1914, to guard American interests.

1904 *Dominican Republic.* January 2 to February 11. American and British naval forces established an area in which no fighting would be allowed and protected American interests in Puerto Plata and Sosua and Santo Domingo City during revolutionary fighting.

1904 *Tangier, Morocco.* "We want either Perdicaris alive or Raisula dead." A squadron demonstrated to force release of a kidnapped American. Marines were landed to protect the consul general.

1904 *Panama.* November 17 to 24. U.S. forces protected American lives and property at Ancon at the time of a threatened insurrection.

1904-05 *Korea.* January 5, 1904, to November 11, 1905. A guard of Marines was sent to protect the American legation in Seoul during the Russo-Japanese War.

1906-09 *Cuba.* September 1906 to January 23, 1909. U.S. forces sought to restore order, protect foreigners, and establish a stable government after serious revolutionary activity.

1907 *Honduras.* March 18 to June 8. To protect American interests during a war between Honduras and Nicaragua, troops were stationed in Trujillo, Ceiba, Puerto Cortez, San Pedro, Laguna and Choloma.

1910 *Nicaragua.* May 19 to September 4. U.S. forces protected American interests at Bluefields.

1911 *Honduras.* January 26. American naval detachments were landed to protect American lives and interests during a civil war in Honduras.

1911 *China.* As the nationalist revolution approached, in October an ensign and 10 men tried to enter Wuchang to rescue missionaries but retired on being warned away, and a small landing force guarded American private property and consulate at Hankow. Marines were deployed in November to guard the cable stations at Shanghai; landing forces were sent for protection in Nanking, Chinkiang, Taku and elsewhere.

1912 *Honduras.* A small force landed to prevent seizure by the government of an American-owned railroad at Puerto Cortez. The forces were withdrawn after the United States disapproved the action.

1912 *Panama.* Troops, on request of both political parties, supervised elections outside the Canal Zone.

1912 *Cuba.* June 5 to August 5. U.S. forces protected American interests on the Province of Oriente, and in Havana.

1912 *China.* August 24 to 26, on Kentucky Island, and August 26 to 30 at Camp Nicholson. U.S. forces protected Americans and American interests during revolutionary activity.

1912 *Turkey.* November 18 to December 3. U.S. forces guarded the American legation at Constantinople during a Balkan War.

19 12-25 *Nicaragua.* August to November 1912. U.S. forces protected American interests during an attempted revolution. A small force, serving as a legation guard and seeking to promote peace and stability, remained until August 5, 1925.

1912-41 *China.* The disorders which began with the overthrow of the dynasty during Kuomintang rebellion in 1912, which were redirected by the invasion of China by Japan, led to demonstrations and landing parties for the protection of U.S. interests in China continuously and at many points from 1912 on to 1941. The guard at Peking and along the route to the sea was maintained until 1941. In 1927, the United States had 5,670 troops ashore in China and 44 naval vessels in its waters. In 1933 the United States had 3,027 armed men ashore. The protective action was generally based on treaties with China concluded from 1858 to 1901.

1913 *Mexico.* September 5 to 7. A few marines landed at Ciaris Estero to aid in evacuating American citizens and others from the Yaqui Valley, made dangerous for foreigners by civil strife.

1914 *Haiti.* January 29 to February 9, February 20 to 21, October 19. Intermittently U.S. naval forces protected American nationals in a time of rioting and revolution.

1914 *Dominican Republic.* June and July. During a revolutionary movement, United States naval forces by gunfire stopped the bombardment of Puerto Plata, and by threat of force maintained Santo Domingo City as a neutral zone.

19 14-17 *Mexico.* Undeclared Mexican-American hostilities followed the Dolphin affair and Villa's raids and included capture of Vera Cruz and later Pershing's expedition into northern Mexico.

19 15-34 *Haiti.* July 28, 1915, to August 15, 1934. U.S. forces maintained order during a period of chronic political instability.

1916 *China.* American forces landed to quell a riot taking place on American property in Nanking.

19 16-24 *Dominican Republic.* May 1916 to September 1924. American naval forces maintained order during a period of chronic and threatened insurrection.

1917 *China.* American troops were landed at Chungking to protect American lives during a political crisis.

1917-18 *World War I. On April 6, 1917, the United States declared war with Germany and on December 7, 1917, with Austria-Hungary.*

Entrance of the United States into the war was precipitated by Germany's submarine warfare against neutral shipping.

1917-22 *Cuba.* U.S. forces protected American interests during an insurrection and subsequent unsettled conditions. Most of the United States armed forces left Cuba by August 1919, but two companies remained at Camaguey until February 1922.

19 18-19 *Mexico.* After withdrawal of the Pershing expedition, U.S. troops entered Mexico in pursuit of bandits at least three times in 1918 and six times in 1919. In August 1918 American and Mexican troops fought at Nogales.

19 18-20 *Panama.* U.S. forces were used for police duty according to treaty stipulations, at Chiriqui, during election disturbances and subsequent unrest.

1918-20 *Soviet Russia.* Marines were landed at and near Vladivostok in June and July to protect the American consulate and other points in the fighting between the Bolshevik troops and the Czech Army which had traversed Siberia from the western front. A joint proclamation of emergency government and neutrality was issued by the American, Japanese, British, French, and Czech commanders in July. In August 7,000 men were landed in Vladivostok and remained until January 1920, as part of an allied occupation force. In September 1918, 5,000 American troops joined the allied intervention force at Archangel and remained until June 1919. These operations were in response to the Bolshevik revolution in Russia and were partly supported by Czarist or Kerensky elements.

1919 *Dalmatia.* U.S. forces were landed at Trau at the request of Italian authorities to police order between the Italians and Serbs.

1919 *Turkey.* Marines from the *U.S.S. Arizona* were landed to guard the U.S. Consulate during the Greek occupation of Constantinople.

1919 *Honduras.* September 8 to 12. A landing force was sent ashore to maintain order in a neutral zone during an attempted revolution.

1920 *China.* March 14. A landing force was sent ashore for a few hours to protect lives during a disturbance at Kiukiang.

1920 *Guatemala.* April 9 to 27. U.S. forces protected the American Legation and other American interests, such as the cable station, during a period of fighting between Unionists and the Government of Guatemala.

1920-22 *Russia (Siberia).* February 16, 1920, to November 19, 1922. A Marine guard was sent to protect the United States radio station and property on Russian Island, Bay of Vladivostok.

1921 *Panama - Costa Rica.* American naval squadrons demonstrated in April on both sides of the Isthmus to prevent war between the two countries over a boundary dispute.

1922 *Turkey.* September and October. A landing force was sent ashore with consent of both Greek and Turkish authorities, to protect American lives and property when the Turkish Nationalists entered Smyrna.

1922-23 *China.* Between April 1922 and November 1923 marines were landed five times to protect Americans during periods of unrest.

1924 *Honduras.* February 28 to March 31, September 10 to 15. U.S. forces protected American lives and interests during election hostilities.

1924 *China.* September. Marines were landed to protect Americans and other foreigners in Shanghai during Chinese factional hostilities.

1925 *China.* January 15 to August 29. Fighting of Chinese factions accompanied by riots and demonstrations in Shanghai brought the landing of American forces to protect lives and property in the International Settlement.

1925 *Honduras.* April 19 to 21. U.S. forces protected foreigners at La Ceiba during a political upheaval.

1925 *Panama.* October 12 to 23. Strikes and rent riots led to the landing of about 600 American troops to keep order and protect American interests.

1926-33 *Nicaragua.* May 7 to June 5, 1926; August 27, 1926 to January 3.

1933. The coup d'etat of General Chamorro aroused revolutionary activities leading to the landing of American marines to protect the interests of the United States. United States forces came and went intermittently until January 3, 1933.

1926 *China.* August and September. The Nationalist attack on Hankow brought the landing of American naval forces to protect American citizens. A small guard was maintained at the consulate general even after September 16, when the rest of the forces were withdrawn. Likewise, when Nationalist forces captured Kiukiang, naval forces were landed for the protection of foreigners November 4 to 6.

1927 *China.* February. Fighting at Shanghai caused American naval forces and marines to be increased. In March a naval guard was stationed at the American consulate at Nanking after Nationalist forces captured the city. American and British destroyers later used shell fire to protect Americans and other foreigners. Subsequently additional forces of marines and naval vessels were stationed in the vicinity of Shanghai and Tientsin.

1932 *China.* American forces were landed to protect American interests during the Japanese occupation of Shanghai.

1933 *Cuba.* During a revolution against President Gerardo Machado naval forces demonstrated but no landing was made.

1934 *China.* Marines landed at Foochow to protect the American Consulate.

1940 *Newfoundland, Bermuda, St. Lucia, Bahamas, Jamaica, Antigua, Trinidad, and British Guiana.* Troops were sent to guard air and naval bases obtained by negotiation with Great Britain. These were sometimes called lend-lease bases.

1941 *Greenland.* Greenland was taken under protection of the United States in April.

1941 *Netherlands (Dutch Guiana).* In November the President ordered American troops to occupy Dutch Guiana, but by agreement with the Netherlands government in exile, Brazil cooperated to protect aluminum ore supply from the bauxite mines in Surinam.

1941 *Iceland.* Iceland was taken under the protection of the United States, with consent of its government, for strategic reasons.

1941 *Germany.* Sometime in the spring the President ordered the Navy to patrol ship lanes to Europe. By July U.S. warships were convoying and by September were attacking German submarines. In November, the Neutrality Act was partly repealed to protect U.S. military aid to Britain.

1941-45 *World War II. On December 8, 1941, the United States declared war with Japan, on December 11 with Germany and Italy, and on June 5, 1942, with Bulgaria, Hungary and Rumania.* The United States declared war against Japan after the surprise bombing of Pearl Harbor, and against Germany and Italy after those nations, under the dictators Hitler and Mussolini, declared war against the United States. The U.S. declared war against

Bulgaria, Hungary and Rumania in response to the declarations of war by those nations against the United States.

1945 *China.* In October 50,000 U.S. Marines were sent to North China to assist Chinese Nationalist authorities in disarming and repatriating the Japanese in China and in controlling ports, railroads, and airfields. This was in addition to approximately 60,000 U.S. forces remaining in China at the end of World War II.

1946 *Trieste.* President Truman ordered the augmentation of U.S. troops along the zonal occupation line and the reinforcement of air forces in northern Italy after Yugoslav forces shot down an unarmed U.S. Army transport plane flying over Venezia Giulia. Earlier U.S. naval units had been dispatched to the scene.

1948 *Palestine.* A marine consular guard was sent to Jerusalem to protect the U.S. Consul General.

1948 *Berlin.* After the Soviet Union established a land blockade of the U.S., British, and French sectors of Berlin on June 24, 1948, the United States and its allies airlifted supplies to Berlin until after the blockade was lifted in May 1949.

1948-49 *China.* Marines were dispatched to Nanking to protect the American Embassy when the city fell to Communist troops, and to Shanghai to aid in the protection and evacuation of Americans.

1950-53 *Korean War.* The United States responded to North Korean invasion of South Korea by going to its assistance, pursuant to United Nations Security Council resolutions. U.S. forces deployed in Korea exceeded 300,000 during the last year of the conflict. Over 36,600 U.S. military were killed in action.

1950-55 *Formosa (Taiwan).* In June 1950 at the beginning of the Korean War, President Truman ordered the U.S. Seventh Fleet to prevent Chinese Communist attacks upon Formosa and Chinese Nationalist operations against mainland China.

1954-55 *China.* Naval units evacuated U.S. civilians and military personnel from the Tachen Islands.

1956 *Egypt.* A marine battalion evacuated U.S. nationals and other persons from Alexandria during the Suez crisis.

1958 *Lebanon.* Marines were landed in Lebanon at the invitation of its government to help protect against threatened insurrection supported from the outside. The President's action was supported by a Congressional resolution passed in 1957 that authorized such actions in that area of the world.

1959-60 *The Caribbean.* 2d Marine Ground Task Force was deployed to protect U.S. nationals during the Cuban crisis.

1962 *Thailand.* The 3d Marine Expeditionary Unit landed on May 17, 1962 to support that country during the threat of Communist pressure from outside; by July 30 the 5,000 marines had been withdrawn.

1962 *Cuba.* On October 22, President Kennedy instituted a "quarantine" on the shipment of offensive missiles to Cuba from the Soviet Union. He also warned the Soviet Union that the launching of any missile from Cuba against any nation in the Western Hemisphere would bring about U.S. nuclear retaliation on the Soviet Union. A negotiated settlement was achieved in a few days.

1962-75 *Laos.* From October 1962 until 1975, the United States played an important role in military support of anti-Communist forces in Laos.

1964 *Congo.* The United States sent four transport planes to provide airlift for Congolese troops during a rebellion and to transport Belgian paratroopers to rescue foreigners.

1964-73 *Vietnam War.* U.S. military advisers had been in South Vietnam for a decade, and their numbers had been increased as the military position of the Saigon government became weaker. After citing what he termed were attacks on U.S. destroyers in the Tonkin Gulf, President Johnson asked in August 1964 for a resolution expressing U.S. determination to support freedom and protect peace in Southeast Asia. Congress responded with the Tonkin Gulf Resolution, expressing support for "all necessary measures" the President might take to repel armed attack against U.S. forces and prevent further aggression. Following this resolution, and following a Communist attack on a U.S. installation in central Vietnam, the United States escalated its participation in the war to a peak of 543,000 military personnel by April 1969.

1965 *Dominican Republic.* The United States intervened to protect lives and property during a Dominican revolt and sent more troops as fears grew that the revolutionary forces were coming increasingly under Communist control.

1967 *Congo.* The United States sent three military transport aircraft with crews to provide the Congo central government with logistical support during a revolt.

1970 *Cambodia.* U.S. troops were ordered into Cambodia to clean out Communist sanctuaries from which Viet Cong and North Vietnamese attacked U.S. and South Vietnamese forces in Vietnam. The object of this attack, which lasted from April 30 to June 30, was to ensure the continuing safe withdrawal of American forces from South Vietnam and to assist the program of Vietnamization.

1974 *Evacuation from Cyprus.* United States naval forces evacuated U.S. civilians during hostilities between Turkish and Greek Cypriot forces.

1975 *Evacuation from Vietnam.* On April 3, 1975, President Ford reported U.S. naval vessels, helicopters, and marines had been sent to assist in evacuation of refugees and U.S. nationals from Vietnam.[2]

1975 *Evacuation from Cambodia.* On April 12, 1975, President Ford reported that he had ordered U.S. military forces to proceed with the planned evacuation of U.S. citizens from Cambodia.

1975 *South Vietnam.* On April 30, 1975, President Ford reported that a force of 70 evacuation helicopters and 865 marines had evacuated about 1,400 U.S. citizens and 5,500 third country nationals and South Vietnamese from landing zones near the U.S. Embassy in Saigon and the Tan Son Nhut Airfield.

1975 *Mayaguez incident.* On May 15, 1975, President Ford reported he had ordered military forces to retake the *SS Mayaguez*, a merchant vessel en route from Hong Kong to Thailand with a U.S. citizen crew which was seized by Cambodian naval patrol boats in international waters and forced to proceed to a nearby island.

1976 *Lebanon.* On July 22 and 23, 1974, helicopters from five U.S. naval vessels evacuated approximately 250 Americans and Europeans from Lebanon during fighting between Lebanese

---

[2] This and subsequent mentions of Presidential reports or notifications refer to reports the President has submitted to Congress related to the War Powers Resolution (P.L. 91-148, November 7, 1973). For a discussion of the War Powers Resolution and various types of reports required under it, see CRS Report RL33532, War Powers Resolution: Presidential Compliance, by Richard F. Grimmett.

factions after an overland convoy evacuation had been blocked by hostilities.

1976 *Korea.* Additional forces were sent to Korea after two American soldiers were killed by North Korean soldiers in the demilitarized zone between North and South Korea while cutting down a tree.

1978 *Zaire.* From May 19 through June 1978, the United States utilized military transport aircraft to provide logistical support to Belgian and French rescue operations in Zaire.

1980 *Iran.* On April 26, 1980, President Carter reported the use of six U.S. transport planes and eight helicopters in an unsuccessful attempt to rescue American hostages being held in Iran.

1981 *El Salvador.* After a guerilla offensive against the government of El Salvador, additional U.S. military advisers were sent to El Salvador, bringing the total to approximately 55, to assist in training government forces in counterinsurgency.

1981 *Libya.* On August 19, 1981, U.S. planes based on the carrier *U.S.S. Nimitz* shot down two Libyan jets over the Gulf of Sidra after one of the Libyan jets had fired a heat-seeking missile. The United States periodically held freedom of navigation exercises in the Gulf of Sidra, claimed by Libya as territorial waters but considered international waters by the United States.

1982 *Sinai.* On March 19, 1982, President Reagan reported the deployment of military personnel and equipment to participate in the Multinational Force and Observers in the Sinai. Participation had been authorized by the Multinational Force and Observers Resolution, P.L. 97-132.

1982 *Lebanon.* On August 21, 1982, President Reagan reported the dispatch of 80 marines to serve in the multinational force to assist in the withdrawal of members of the Palestine Liberation force from Beirut. The Marines left September 20, 1982.

1982-1983 *Lebanon.* On September 29, 1982, President Reagan reported the deployment of 1200 marines to serve in a temporary multinational force to facilitate the restoration of Lebanese government sovereignty. On Sept. 29, 1983, Congress passed the Multinational Force in Lebanon Resolution (P.L. 98-119) authorizing the continued participation for eighteen months.

1983 *Egypt.* After a Libyan plane bombed a city in Sudan on March 18, 1983, and Sudan and Egypt appealed for assistance, the

United States dispatched an AWACS electronic surveillance plane to Egypt.

1983-89 *Honduras.* In July 1983 the United States undertook a series of exercises in Honduras that some believed might lead to conflict with Nicaragua. On March 25, 1986, unarmed U.S. military helicopters and crewmen ferried Honduran troops to the Nicaraguan border to repel Nicaraguan troops.

1983 *Chad.* On August 8, 1983, President Reagan reported the deployment of two AWACS electronic surveillance planes and eight F-15 fighter planes and ground logistical support forces to assist Chad against Libyan and rebel forces.

1983 *Grenada.* On October 25, 1983, President Reagan reported a landing on Grenada by Marines and Army airborne troops to protect lives and assist in the restoration of law and order and at the request of five members of the Organization of Eastern Caribbean States.

1984 *Persian Gulf.* On June 5, 1984, Saudi Arabian jet fighter planes, aided by intelligence from a U.S. AWACS electronic surveillance aircraft and fueled by a U.S. KC-10 tanker, shot down two Iranian fighter planes over an area of the Persian Gulf proclaimed as a protected zone for shipping.

1985 *Italy.* On October 10, 1985, U.S. Navy pilots intercepted an Egyptian airliner and forced it to land in Sicily. The airliner was carrying the hijackers of the Italian cruise ship *Achille Lauro* who had killed an American citizen during the hijacking.

1986 *Libya.* On March 26, 1986, President Reagan reported to Congress that, on March 24 and 25, U.S. forces, while engaged in freedom of navigation exercises around the Gulf of Sidra, had been attacked by Libyan missiles and the United States had responded with missiles.

1986 *Libya.* On April 16, 1986, President Reagan reported that U.S. air and naval forces had conducted bombing strikes on terrorist facilities and military installations in Libya.

1986 *Bolivia.* U.S. Army personnel and aircraft assisted Bolivia in anti-drug operations.

1987-88 *Persian Gulf.* After the Iran-Iraq War resulted in several military incidents in the Persian Gulf, the United States increased U.S. joint military forces operations in the Persian Gulf and adopted a policy of reflagging and escorting Kuwaiti oil tankers through the Gulf. President Reagan reported that U.S. Navy ships had been fired upon or struck mines or taken other military action on September 23, October 10, and October 20, 1987 and April 19, July 4, and July 14, 1988. The United States gradually reduced its forces after a cease-fire between Iran and Iraq on August 20, 1988.

1988 *Panama.* In mid-March and April 1988, during a period of instability in Panama and as pressure grew for Panamanian military leader General Manuel Noriega to resign, the United States sent 1,000 troops to Panama, to "further safeguard the canal, U.S. lives, property and interests in the area." The forces supplemented 10,000 U.S. military personnel already in Panama.

1989 *Libya.* On January 4, 1989, two U.S. Navy F-14 aircraft based on the *U.S.S. John F. Kennedy* shot down two Libyan jet fighters over the Mediterranean Sea about 70 miles north of Libya. The U.S. pilots said the Libyan planes had demonstrated hostile intentions.

1989 *Panama.* On May 11, 1989, in response to General Noriega's disregard of the results of the Panamanian election, President Bush ordered a brigade-sized force of approximately 1,900 troops to augment the estimated 11,000 U.S. forces already in the area.

1989 *Andean Initiative in War on Drugs.* On September 15, 1989, President Bush announced that military and law enforcement assistance would be sent to help the Andean nations of Colombia, Bolivia, and Peru combat illicit drug producers and traffickers. By mid-September there were 50-100 U.S. military advisers in Colombia in connection with transport and training in the use of military equipment, plus seven Special Forces teams of 2-12 persons to train troops in the three countries.

1989 *Philippines.* On December 2, 1989, President Bush reported that on December 1 U.S. fighter planes from Clark Air Base in the Philippines had assisted the Aquino government to repel a coup attempt. In addition, 100 marines were sent from the U.S. Navy base at Subic Bay to protect the U.S. Embassy in Manila.

1989-90 *Panama.* On December 21, 1989, President Bush reported that he had ordered U.S. military forces to Panama to protect the lives of American citizens and bring General Noriega to justice. By February 13, 1990, all the invasion forces had been withdrawn.

1990 *Liberia.* On August 6, 1990, President Bush reported that a reinforced rifle company had been sent to provide additional security to the U.S. Embassy in Monrovia, and that helicopter teams had evacuated U.S. citizens from Liberia.

1990 *Saudi Arabia.* On August 9, 1990, President Bush reported that he had ordered the forward deployment of substantial elements of the U.S. armed forces into the Persian Gulf region to help defend Saudi Arabia after the August 2 invasion of Kuwait by Iraq. On November 16, 1990, he reported the continued buildup of the forces to ensure an adequate offensive military option.

1991 *Iraq.* On January 18, 1991, President Bush reported that he had directed U.S. armed forces to commence combat operations on January 16 against Iraqi forces and military targets in Iraq and Kuwait, in conjunction with a coalition of allies and U.N. Security Council resolutions. On January 12 Congress had passed the Authorization for Use of Military Force against Iraq Resolution (P.L. 102-1). Combat operations were suspended on February 28, 1991.

1991 *Iraq.* On May 17, 1991, President Bush stated in a status report to Congress that the Iraqi repression of the Kurdish people had necessitated a limited introduction of U.S. forces into northern Iraq for emergency relief purposes.

1991 *Zaire.* On September 25-27, 1991, after widespread looting and rioting broke out in Kinshasa, U.S. Air Force C-141s transported 100 Belgian troops and equipment into Kinshasa. U.S. planes also carried 300 French troops into the Central African Republic and hauled back American citizens and third country nationals from locations outside Zaire.

1992 *Sierra Leone.* On May 3, 1992, U.S. military planes evacuated Americans from Sierra Leone, where military leaders had overthrown the government.

1992 *Kuwait.* On August 3, 1992, the United States began a series of military exercises in Kuwait, following Iraqi refusal to recognize a new border drawn up by the United Nations and refusal to cooperate with U.N. inspection teams.

1992 *Iraq.* On September 16, 1992, President Bush stated in a status report to Congress that he had ordered U.S. participation in the enforcement of a prohibition against Iraqi flights in a specified zone in southern Iraq, and aerial reconnaissance to monitor Iraqi compliance with the cease-fire resolution.

1992 *Somalia.* On December 10, 1992, President Bush reported that he had deployed U.S. armed forces to Somalia in response to a humanitarian crisis and a U.N. Security Council Resolution determining that the situation constituted a threat to international peace. This operation, called Operation Restore Hope, was part of a U.S.-led United Nations Unified Task Force (UNITAF) and came to an end on May 4, 1993. U.S. forces continued to participate in the successor United Nations Operation in Somalia (UNOSOM II), which the U.N. Security Council authorized to assist Somalia in political reconciliation and restoration of peace.

1993 *Iraq.* On January 19, 1993, President Bush said in a status report that on December 27, 1992, U.S. aircraft had shot down an Iraqi aircraft in the prohibited zone; on January 13 aircraft from the United States and coalition partners had attacked missile bases in southern Iraq; and further military actions had occurred on January 17 and 18. Administration officials said the United States was deploying a battalion task force to Kuwait to underline the continuing U.S. commitment to Kuwaiti independence.

1993 *Iraq.* On January 21, 1993, shortly after his inauguration, President Clinton said the United States would continue the Bush policy on Iraq, and U.S. aircraft fired at targets in Iraq after pilots sensed Iraqi radar or anti-aircraft fire directed at them.

1993 *Bosnia.* On February 28, 1993, the United States began an airdrop of relief supplies aimed at Muslims surrounded by Serbian forces in Bosnia.

1993 *Bosnia.* On April 13, 1993, President Clinton reported U.S. forces were participating in a NATO air action to enforce a U.N. ban on all unauthorized military flights over Bosnia-Hercegovina.

1993 *Iraq.* In a status report on Iraq of May 24, President Clinton said that on April 9 and April 18 U.S. planes had bombed or fired missiles at Iraqi anti-aircraft sites that had tracked U.S. aircraft.

1993 *Somalia.* On June 10, 1993, President Clinton reported that in response to attacks against U.N. forces in Somalia by a factional leader, the U.S. Quick Reaction Force in the area had participated in military action to quell the violence. On July 1

President Clinton reported further air and ground military operations on June 12 and June 17 aimed at neutralizing military capabilities that had impeded U.N. efforts to deliver humanitarian relief and promote national reconstruction, and additional instances occurred in the following months.

1993 *Iraq.* On June 28, 1993, President Clinton reported that on June 26 U.S. naval forces had launched missiles against the Iraqi Intelligence Service's headquarters in Baghdad in response to an unsuccessful attempt to assassinate former President Bush in Kuwait in April 1993.

1993 *Iraq.* In a status report of July 22, 1993, President Clinton said on June 19 a U.S. aircraft had fired a missile at an Iraqi anti-aircraft site displaying hostile intent. U.S. planes also bombed an Iraqi missile battery on August 19, 1993.

1993 *Macedonia.* On July 9, 1993, President Clinton reported the deployment of 350 U.S. soldiers to the former Yugoslav Republic of Macedonia to participate in the U.N. Protection Force to help maintain stability in the area of former Yugoslavia.

1993 *Haiti.* On October 20, 1993, President Clinton reported that U.S. ships had begun to enforce a U.N. embargo against Haiti.

1994 *Bosnia.* On February 17, 1994, President Clinton reported that the United States had expanded its participation in United Nations and NATO efforts to reach a peaceful solution to the conflict in former Yugoslavia and that 60 U.S. aircraft were available for participation in the authorized NATO missions.

1994 *Bosnia.* On March 1, 1994, President Clinton reported that on February 28 U.S. planes patrolling the "no-fly zone" in former Yugoslavia under the North Atlantic Treaty Organization (NATO) shot down 4 Serbian Galeb planes.

1994 *Bosnia.* On April 12, 1994, President Clinton reported that on April 10 and 11, U.S. warplanes under NATO command had fired against Bosnian Serb forces shelling the "safe" city of Gorazde.

1994 *Rwanda.* On April 12, 1994, President Clinton reported that combat-equipped U.S. military forces had been deployed to Burundi to conduct possible non-combatant evacuation operations of U.S. citizens and other third-country nationals from Rwanda, where widespread fighting had broken out. By September 30, 1994, all U.S. troops had departed from Rwanda and surrounding nations. In the efense Appropriations Act for FY1995 (P.L. 103-335, signed September 30, 1994), Congress barred use of funds for U.S. military participation in or around Rwanda after October 7, 1994, except for any action necessary to protect U.S. citizens.

1994 *Macedonia.* On April 19, 1994, President Clinton reported that the U.S. contingent in the former Yugoslav Republic of Macedonia had been augmented by a reinforced company of 200 personnel.

1994 *Haiti.* On April 20, 1994, President Clinton reported that U.S. naval forces had continued enforcement of the U.N. embargo in the waters around Haiti and that 712 vessels had been boarded since October 20, 1993.

1994 *Bosnia.* On August 22, 1994, President Clinton reported the use on August 5 of U.S. aircraft under NATO to attack Bosnian Serb heavy weapons in the Sarajevo heavy weapons exclusion zone upon request of the U.N. Protection Forces.

1994 *Haiti.* On September 21, 1994, President Clinton reported the deployment of 1,500 troops to Haiti to restore democracy in Haiti. The troop level was subsequently increased to 20,000.

1994 *Bosnia.* On November 22, 1994, President Clinton reported the use of U.S. combat aircraft on November 21, 1994, under NATO, to attack bases used by Serbs to attack the town of Bihac in Bosnia.

1994 *Macedonia.* On December 22, 1994, President Clinton reported that the U.S. Army contingent in the former Yugoslav Republic of Macedonia continued its peacekeeping mission and that the current contingent would soon be replaced by about 500 soldiers from the 3rd Battalion, 5th Cavalry Regiment, 1st Armored Division from Kirchgons, Germany.

1995 *Somalia.* On March 1, 1995, President Clinton reported that on February 27, 1995, 1,800 combat-equipped U.S. armed forces personnel began deployment into Mogadishu, Somalia, to assist in the withdrawal of U.N. forces assigned there to the United Nations Operation in Somalia (UNOSOM II). This mission was completed on March 3, 1995.

1995 *Haiti.* On March 21, 1995, President Clinton reported that U.S. military forces in Haiti as part of a U.N. Multinational Force had been reduced to just under 5,300 personnel. He noted that as of

March 31, 1995, approximately 2,500 U.S. personnel would remain in Haiti as part of the U.N. Mission in Haiti (UNMIH).

1995 *Bosnia.* On May 24, 1995, President Clinton reported that U.S. combat-equipped fighter aircraft and other aircraft continued to contribute to NATO's enforcement of the no-fly zone in airspace over Bosnia-Herzegovina. U.S. aircraft, he noted, were also available for close air support of U.N. forces in Croatia. Roughly 500 U.S. soldiers continued to be deployed in the former Yugoslav Republic of acedonia as part of the U.N. Preventive Deployment Force (UNPREDEP). U.S. forces continued to support U.N. refugee and embargo operations in this region.

1995 *Bosnia.* On September 1, 1995, President Clinton reported that "U.S. combat and support aircraft" had been used beginning on August 29, 1995, in a series of NATO air strikes against Bosnian Serb Army (BSA) forces in Bosnia-Herzegovina that were threatening the U.N.-declared safe areas of Sarajevo, Tuzla, and Gorazde. He noted that during the first day of operations, "some 300 sorties were flown against 23 targets in the vicinity of Sarajevo, Tuzla, Gorazde and Mostar."

1995 *Haiti.* On September 21, 1995, President Clinton reported that currently the United States had 2,400 military personnel in Haiti as participants in the U.N. Mission in Haiti (UNMIH). In addition, 260 U.S. military personnel were assigned to the U.S. Support Group Haiti.

1995 *Bosnia.* On December 6, 1995, President Clinton reported to Congress, that he had "ordered the deployment of approximately 1,500 U.S. military personnel" to Bosnia-Herzegovina and Croatia as part of a NATO "enabling force" to lay the groundwork for the prompt and safe deployment of the NATO-led Implementation Force (IFOR)," which would be used to implement the Bosnian peace agreement after its signing. The President also noted that he had authorized deployment of roughly 3,000 other U.S. military personnel to Hungary, Italy, and Croatia to establish infrastructure for the enabling force and the IFOR.

1995 *Bosnia.* On December 21, 1995, President Clinton reported to Congress that he had ordered the deployment of approximately 20,000 U.S. military personnel to participate in the NATO-led Implementation Force (IFOR) in the Republic of Bosnia-

Herzegovina, and approximately 5,000 U.S. military personnel would be deployed in other former Yugoslav states, primarily in Croatia. In addition, about 7,000 U.S. support forces would be deployed to Hungary, Italy and Croatia and other regional states in support of IFOR's mission.

1996 *Haiti.* On March 21, 1996, President Clinton reported to Congress that beginning in January 1996 there had been a "phased reduction" in the number of United States personnel assigned to the United Nations Mission in Haiti (UNMIH). As of March 21, 309 U.S. personnel remained a part of UNMIH. These U.S. forces were "equipped for combat."

1996 *Liberia.* On April 11, 1996, President Clinton reported to Congress that on April 9, 1996 due to the "deterioration of the security situation and the resulting threat to American citizens" in Liberia he had ordered U.S. military forces to evacuate from that country "private U.S. citizens and certain third-country nationals who had taken refuge in the U.S. Embassy compound...."

1996 *Liberia.* On May 20, 1996, President Clinton reported to Congress the continued deployment of U.S. military forces in Liberia to evacuate both American citizens and other foreign personnel, and to respond to various isolated "attacks on the American Embassy complex" in Liberia. The President noted that the deployment of U.S. forces would continue until there was no longer any need for enhanced security at the Embassy and a requirement to maintain an evacuation capability in the country.

1996 *Central African Republic.* On May 23, 1996, President Clinton reported to Congress the deployment of U.S. military personnel to Bangui, Central African Republic, to conduct the evacuation from that country of "private U.S. citizens and certain U.S. Government employees," and to provide "enhanced security for the American Embassy in Bangui."

1996 *Bosnia.* On June 21, 1996, President Clinton reported to Congress that United States forces totaling about 17,000 remain deployed in Bosnia "under NATO operational command and control" as part of the NATO Implementation Force (IFOR). In addition, about 5,500 U.S. military personnel were deployed in Hungary, Italy and Croatia, and other regional states to provide "logistical and other support to IFOR." The President noted that it was the intention that IFOR would complete the withdrawal of all troops in the weeks after December 20, 1996, on a schedule "set by NATO commanders consistent with the safety of troops and the logistical requirements for an orderly withdrawal." He also noted that a U.S. Army contingent (of about 500 U.S. soldiers) remained in the Former Yugoslav Republic of Macedonia as part of the United Nations Preventive Deployment Force (UNPREDEP).

1996 *Rwanda and Zaire.* On December 2, 1996, President Clinton reported to Congress that to support the humanitarian efforts of the United Nations regarding refugees in Rwanda and the Great Lakes Region of Eastern Zaire, he had authorized the use of U.S. personnel and aircraft, including AC-130U planes to help in surveying the region in support of humanitarian operations, although fighting still was ccurring in the area, and U.S. aircraft had been subject to fire when on flight duty.

1996 *Bosnia.* On December 20, 1996, President Clinton reported to Congress that he had authorized U.S. participation in an IFOR follow-on force in Bosnia, known as SFOR (Stabilization Force), under NATO command. The President said the U.S. forces contribution to SFOR was to be "about 8,500" personnel whose primary mission is to deter or prevent a resumption of hostilities or new threats to peace in Bosnia. SFOR's duration in Bosnia is expected to be 18 months, with progressive reductions and eventual withdrawal.

1997 *Albania.* On March 15, 1997, President Clinton reported to Congress that on March 13, 1997, he had utilized U.S. military forces to evacuate certain U.S. Government employees and private U.S. citizens from Tirana, Albania, and to enhance security for the U.S. Embassy in that city.

1997 *Congo and Gabon.* On March 27, 1997, President Clinton reported to Congress that, on March 25, 1997, a standby evacuation force of U.S. military personnel had been deployed to Congo and Gabon to provide enhanced security for American private citizens, government employees, and selected third country nationals in Zaire, and to be available for any necessary evacuation operation.

1997 *Sierra Leone.* On May 30, 1997, President Clinton reported to Congress that on May 29 and May 30, 1997, U.S. military personnel were deployed to Freetown, Sierra Leone, to prepare for and undertake the evacuation of certain U.S. government employees and private U.S. citizens.

1997 *Bosnia.* On June 20, 1997, President Clinton reported to Congress that U.S. Armed Forces continued to support peacekeeping operations in Bosnia and other states in the region in support of the NATO-led Stabilization Force (SFOR). He reported that currently most U.S. military personnel involved in SFOR were in Bosnia, near Tuzla, and about 2,800 U.S. troops were deployed in Hungary, Croatia, Italy, and other regional states to provide logistics and other support to SFOR. A U.S. Army continent of about 500 also remained in the Former Yugoslav Republic of Macedonia as part of the U.N. Preventive Deployment Force (UNPREDEP).

1997 *Cambodia.* On July 11, 1997, President Clinton reported to Congress that in an effort to ensure the security of American citizens in Cambodia during a period of domestic conflict there, he had deployed a Task Force of about 550 U.S. military personnel to Utapao Air Base in Thailand. These personnel were to be available for possible emergency evacuation operations in Cambodia as deemed necessary.

1997 *Bosnia.* On December 19, 1997, President Clinton reported to Congress that he intended "in principle" to have the United States participate in a security presence in Bosnia when the NATO SFOR contingent withdrew in the summer of 1998.

1998 *Guinea-Bissau.* On June 12, 1998, President Clinton reported to Congress that, on June 10, 1998, in response to an army mutiny in Guinea-Bissau endangering the U.S. Embassy, U.S. government employees and citizens in that country, he had deployed a standby evacuation force of U.S. military personnel to Dakar, Senegal, to remove such individuals, as well as selected third country nationals, from the city of Bissau. The deployment continued until the necessary evacuations were completed.

1998 *Bosnia.* On June 19, 1998, President Clinton reported to Congress regarding activities in the last six months of combat-equipped U.S. forces in support of NATO's SFOR in Bosnia and surrounding areas of former Yugoslavia.

1998 *Kenya and Tanzania.* On August 10, 1998, President Clinton reported to Congress that he had deployed, on August 7, 1998, a Joint Task Force of U.S. military personnel to Nairobi, Kenya, to coordinate the medical and disaster assistance related to the bombings of the U.S. Embassies in Kenya and Tanzania. He also reported that teams of 50-100 security personnel had arrived in Nairobi, Kenya, and Dar es Salaam, Tanzania, to enhance the security of the U.S. Embassies and citizens there.

1998 *Albania.* On August 18, 1998, President Clinton reported to Congress that he had, on August 16, 1998, deployed 200 U.S. Marines and 10 Navy SEALS to the U.S. Embassy compound in Tirana, Albania, to enhance security against reported threats against U.S. personnel.

1998 *Afghanistan and Sudan.* On August 21, 1998, by letter, President Clinton reported to Congress that he had authorized airstrikes on August 20th against camps and installations in Afghanistan and Sudan used by the Osama bin Laden terrorist organization. The President did so based on what he viewed as convincing information that the bin Laden organization was responsible for the bombings, on August 7, 1998, of the U.S. Embassies in Kenya and Tanzania.

1998 *Liberia.* On September 29, 1998, President Clinton reported to Congress that on September 27, 1998 he had, due to political nstability and civil disorder in Liberia, deployed a stand-by response and evacuation force of 30 U.S. military personnel to augment the security force at the U.S. Embassy in Monrovia, and to provide for a rapid evacuation capability, as needed, to remove U.S. citizens and government personnel from the country.

1998 *Iraq.* During the period from December 16-23, 1998, the United States, together with the United Kingdom, conducted a bombing campaign, termed Operation Desert Fox, against Iraqi industrial facilities deemed capable of producing weapons of mass destruction, and against other Iraqi military and security targets.

1998-1999 *Iraq.* Beginning in late December 1998, and continuing during 1999, the United States, together with forces of the coalition enforcing the "no-fly" zones over Iraq, conducted military operations against the Iraqi air defense system on numerous occasions in response to actual or potential threats against aircraft enforcing the "no-fly" zones in northern and southern Iraq.

1999 *Bosnia.* On January 19, 1999, President Clinton reported to Congress that he was continuing to authorize the use of combat-equipped U.S. Armed Forces in Bosnia and other states in the region as participants in and supporters of the NATO-led Stabilization Force (SFOR). He noted that the U.S. SFOR military personnel totaled about 6,900, with about 2,300 U.S. military personnel deployed to Hungary, Croatia, Italy and other regional states. Also some 350 U.S. military personnel remain deployed in the Former Yugoslav Republic of Macedonia (FYROM) as part of the U.N. Preventive Deployment Force (UNPREDEP).

1999 *Kenya.* On February 25, 1999, President Clinton reported to Congress that he was continuing to deploy U.S. military personnel in that country to assist in providing security for the U.S. embassy and American citizens in Nairobi, pending completion of renovations of the American embassy facility in Nairobi, subject of a terrorist bombing in August 1998.

1999 *Yugoslavia.* On March 26, 1999, President Clinton reported to Congress that, on March 24, 1999, U.S. military forces, at his direction, and in coalition with NATO allies, had commenced air strikes against Yugoslavia in response to the Yugoslav government's campaign of violence and repression against the ethnic Albanian population in Kosovo.

1999 *Yugoslavia/Albania.* On April 7, 1999, President Clinton reported to Congress, that he had ordered additional U.S. military forces to Albania, including rotary wing aircraft, artillery, and tactical missiles systems to enhance NATO's ability to conduct effective air operations in Yugoslavia. About 2,500 soldiers and aviators are to be deployed as part of this task force. The President also reported the deployment of U.S. military forces to Albania and Macedonia to support humanitarian disaster relief operations for Kosovar refugees.

1999 *Yugoslavia/Albania.* On May 25, 1999, President Clinton reported to Congress, "consistent with the war Powers Resolution" that he had directed "deployment of additional aircraft and forces to support NATO's ongoing efforts [against Yugoslavia], including several thousand additional U.S. Armed Forces personnel to Albania in support of the deep strike force located there." He also directed that additional U.S. forces be deployed to the region to assist in "humanitarian operations."

1999 *Yugoslavia/Kosovo.* On June 12, 1999, President Clinton reported to Congress, "consistent with the War Powers Resolution" that he had directed the deployment of about "7,000 U.S. military personnel as the U.S. contribution to the approximately 50,000-member, NATO-led security force (KFOR)" currently being assembled in Kosovo. He also noted that about "1,500 U.S. military personnel, under separate U.S. command and control, will deploy to other countries in the region, as our national support element, in support of KFOR."

1999 *Bosnia.* On July 19, 1999, President Clinton reported to Congress "consistent with the War Powers Resolution" that about 6,200 U.S. military personnel were continuing to participate in the NATO-led Stabilization Force (SFOR) in Bosnia, and that another 2,200 personnel were supporting SFOR operations from Hungary, Croatia, and Italy. He also noted that U.S. military personnel remain in the Former Yugoslav Republic of Macedonia to support the international security presence in Kosovo (KFOR).

1999 *East Timor.* On October 8, 1999, President Clinton reported to Congress "consistent with the War Powers Resolution" that he had directed the deployment of a limited number of U.S. military forces to East Timor to support the U.N. multinational force (INTERFET) aimed at restoring peace to East Timor. U.S. support has been limited initially to "communications, logistics, planning assistance and transportation." The President further noted that he had authorized deployment of the amphibious ship USS BELLEAU WOOD, together with its helicopters and her complement of personnel from the 31st Marine Expeditionary Unit (Special Operations Capable) (MEU SOC) to the East Timor region, to provide helicopter airlift and search and rescue support to the multinational operation. U.S. participation was anticipated to continue until the transition to a U.N. peacekeeping operation was complete.

1999 *Yugoslavia/Kosovo.* On December 15, 1999, President Clinton reported to Congress "consistent with the War Powers Resolution" that U.S. combat-equipped military personnel continued to serve as part of the NATO-led security force in Kosovo (KFOR). He noted that the American contribution to KFOR in Kosovo was "approximately 8,500 U.S. military personnel."U.S. forces were deployed in a sector centered around "Urosevac in the eastern portion of Kosovo." For U.S. KFOR forces, "maintaining public security is a key task." Other U.S. military personnel are deployed to other countries in the region to serve in administrative and logistics support roles for U.S. forces in KFOR. Of these forces, about 1,500 U.S. military personnel are in Macedonia and Greece, and occasionally in Albania.

1999-2000 *Iraq.* At various times during 1999, and continuing throughout 2000 the United States, together with forces of the coalition enforcing the "no-fly" zones over Iraq, conducted military operations against the Iraqi air defense system on numerous occasions in response to actual or potential threats against aircraft enforcing the "no-fly" zones in northern and southern Iraq.

2000 *Bosnia.* On January 25, 2000, President Clinton reported to Congress "consistent with the War Powers Resolution" that the U.S. continued to provide combat-equipped U.S. Armed Forces to Bosnia-Herzegovina and other states in the region as part of the NATO led Stabilization Force (SFOR). The President noted that the U.S. force contribution was being reduced from "approximately 6,200 to 4,600 personnel," with the U.S. forces assigned to Multinational Division, North, centered around the city of Tuzla. He added that approximately 1,500 U.S. military personnel were deployed to Hungary, Croatia, and Italy to provide "logistical and other support to SFOR," and that U.S. forces continue to support SFOR in "efforts to apprehend persons indicted for war crimes."

2000 *East Timor.* On February 25, 2000, President Clinton reported to Congress "consistent with the War Powers Resolution" that he had authorized the participation of a small number of U.S. military personnel in support of the United Nations Transitional Administration in East Timor (UNTAET), which has a mandate to maintain law and order throughout East Timor, and to facilitate establishment of an effective administration there, delivery of humanitarian assistance and support the building of self-government. The President reported that the U.S. contingent was small: three military observers, and one judge advocate. To facilitate and coordinate U.S. military activities in East Timor, the President also authorized the deployment of a support group (US GET), consisting of 30 U.S. personnel. U.S. personnel would be temporarily deployed to East Timor, on a rotational basis, and through periodic ship visits, during which U.S. forces would conduct "humanitarian and assistance activities throughout East Timor." Rotational activities should continue through the summer of 2000.

2000 *Sierra Leone.* On May 12, 2000, President Clinton, "consistent with the War Powers Resolution" reported to Congress that he had ordered a U.S. Navy patrol craft to deploy to Sierra Leone to be ready to support evacuation operations from that country if needed. He also authorized a U.S. C-17 aircraft to deliver "ammunition, and other supplies and equipment" to Sierra Leone in support of United Nations peacekeeping operations there.

2000 *Yugoslavia/Kosovo.* On June 16, 2000, President Clinton reported to Congress, "consistent with the War Powers Resolution," that the U.S. was continuing to provide military personnel to the NATO-led KFOR security force in Kosovo. U.S. forces were numbered at 7,500, but were scheduled to be reduced to 6,000 when ongoing troop rotations were completed. U.S. forces in Kosovo are assigned to a sector centered near Gnjilane in eastern Kosovo. Other U.S. military personnel are deployed to other countries serving in administrative and logistics support roles, with approximately 1,000 U.S. personnel in Macedonia, Albania and Greece.

2000 *Bosnia.* On July 25, 2000, President Clinton reported to Congress, "consistent with the War Powers Resolution," that combat-equipped U.S. military personnel continued to participate in the NATO-led Stabilization Force (SFOR) in Bosnia-Herzegovina, being deployed to Bosnia, and other states in the region in support of peacekeeping efforts in former Yugoslavia. U.S. military personnel levels have been reduced from 6,200 to 4,600. Apart from the forces in Bosnia, approximately 1,000 U.S. personnel continue to be deployed in support roles in Hungary, Croatia, and Italy.

2000 *East Timor.* On August 25, 2000, President Clinton reported to Congress,"consistent with the War Powers Resolution," that the United States was currently contributing three military observers to the United Nations Transitional Administration in East Timor (UNTAET) that is charged by the U.N. with restoring and maintaining peace and security there. He also noted that the U.S. was maintaining a military presence in East Timor separate from UNTAET, comprised of about 30 U.S. personnel who facilitate and coordinate U.S. military activities in East Timor and rotational operations of U.S. forces there. U.S. forces currently conduct humanitarian and civic assistance activities for East Timor's citizens. U.S. rotational presence operations in East Timor are presently expected, the President said, to continue through December 2000.

2000 *Yemen.* On October 14, 2000, President Clinton reported to Congress, "consistent with the War Powers Resolution," that on October 12, 2000, in the wake of an attack on the USS COLE in the port of Aden, Yemen, he had authorized deployment of about 45 military personnel from U.S. Naval Forces Central Command to Aden to provide "medical, security, and disaster response assistance." The President further reported that on October 13, 2000 about 50 U.S. military security personnel arrived in Aden, and that additional "security elements" may be deployed to the area, to enhance the ability of the U.S. to ensure the security of the USS COLE and the personnel responding to the incident. In addition, two U.S. Navy surface combatant vessels are operating in or near Yemeni territorial waters to provide communications and other support, as required.

2000 *Yugoslavia/Kosovo.* On December 18, 2000, President Clinton reported to Congress, "consistent with the War Powers Resolution," that the United States was continuing to provide approximately 5,600 U.S. military personnel in support of peacekeeping efforts in Kosovo as part of the NATO-led international security force in Kosovo (KFOR). An additional 500 U.S. military personnel are deployed as the National Support Element in Macedonia, with an occasional presence in Albania and Greece. U.S. forces are assigned to a sector centered around

Gnjilane in the eastern portion of Kosovo. The President noted that the mission for these U.S. military forces is maintaining a safe and secure environment through conducting "security patrols in urban areas and in the countryside throughout their sector."

2001 *East Timor.* On March 2, 2001, President George W. Bush reported to Congress, "consistent with the War Powers Resolution," that U. S. armed forces were continuing to support the United Nations peacekeeping effort in East Timor aimed at providing security and maintaining law and order in East Timor, coordinating delivery of humanitarian assistance, and helping establish the basis for self-government in East Timor. The U.S. currently has three military observers attached to the United Nations Transitional Administration in East Timor (UNTAET). The United States also has a separate military presence, the U.S. Support Group East Timor (USGET), of approximately 12 U.S. personnel, including a security detachment, which "facilitates and coordinates" U.S. military activities in East Timor.

2001 *Yugoslavia/Kosovo.* On May 18, 2001, President George W. Bush reported to Congress, "consistent with the War Powers Resolution,"that the United States was continuing to provide approximately 6,000 U.S. military personnel in support of peacekeeping efforts in Kosovo as part of the NATO-led international security force in Kosovo (KFOR). An additional 500 U.S. military personnel are deployed as the National Support Element in Macedonia, with an occasional presence in Greece and Albania. U.S. forces in Kosovo are assigned to a sector centered around Gnjilane in the eastern portion. President Bush noted that the mission for these U.S. military forces is maintaining a safe and secure environment through conducting security patrols in urban areas and in the countryside through their sector.

2001 *Bosnia.* On July 25, 2001, President George W. Bush reported to Congress, "consistent with the War Powers Resolution, about 3,800 combat-equipped U.S. Armed Forces continued to be deployed in Bosnia-Herzegovina, and other regional states as part of the NATO-led Stabilization Force (SFOR). Most were based at Tuzla in Bosnia. About 500 others were based in

Hungary, Croatia, and Italy, providing logistical and other support.

2001 *Iraq.* At various times throughout 2001, the United States, together with forces of the coalition enforcing the "no-fly" zones over Iraq, conducted military operations against the Iraqi air defense system on numerous occasions in response to actual or potential threats against aircraft enforcing the "no-fly" zones in northern and southern Iraq.

2001 *East Timor.* On August 31, 2001, President George W. Bush reported to Congress, "consistent with the War Powers Resolution," that U. S. armed forces were continuing to support the United Nations peacekeeping effort in East Timor aimed at providing security and maintaining law and order in East Timor, coordinating delivery of humanitarian assistance, and helping establish the basis for self-government in East Timor. The U.S. currently has three military observers attached to the United Nations Transitional Administration in East Timor (UNTAET). The United States also has a separate military presence, the U.S. Support Group East Timor (USGET), of approximately 20 U.S. personnel, including a security detachment, which "facilitates and coordinates" U.S. military activities in East Timor, as well as a rotational presence of U.S. forces through temporary deployments to East Timor. The President stated that U.S. forces would continue a presence through December 2001, while options for a U.S. presence in 2002 are being reviewed, with the President's objective being redeployment of USGET personnel, as circumstances permit.

2001 *Terrorism threat.* On September 24, 2001, President George W. Bush reported to Congress, "consistent with the War Powers Resolution," and "Senate Joint Resolution 23" that in response to terrorist attacks on the World Trade Center and the Pentagon he had ordered the "deployment of various combat-equipped and combat support forces to a number of foreign nations in the Central and Pacific Command areas of operations." The President noted in efforts to "prevent and deter terrorism" he might find it necessary to order additional forces into these and other areas of the world...." He stated that he could not now predict "the scope and duration of these deployments," or the "actions necessary to counter the terrorist threat to the United States."

2001 *Afghanistan.* On October 9, 2001, President George W. Bush reported to Congress, "consistent with the War Powers Resolution," and "Senate Joint Resolution 23" that on October 7, 2001, U.S. Armed Forces "began combat action in Afghanistan against Al Qaida terrorists and their Taliban supporters." The President stated that he had directed this military action in response to the September 11, 2001 attacks on U.S. "territory, our citizens, and our way of life, and to the continuing threat of terrorist acts against the United States and our friends and allies."This military action was "part of our campaign against terrorism" and was "designed to disrupt the use of Afghanistan as a terrorist base of operations."

2001 *Yugoslavia/Kosovo.* On November 19, 2001, President George W. Bush reported to Congress, "consistent with the War Powers Resolution," that the United States was continuing to provide approximately 5,500 U.S. military personnel in support of eacekeeping efforts in Kosovo as part of the NATO-led international security force in Kosovo (KFOR). An additional 500 U.S. military personnel are deployed as the National Support Element in Macedonia, with an occasional presence in Greece and Albania. U.S. forces in Kosovo are assigned to a sector centered around Gnjilane in the eastern portion. President Bush noted that the mission for these U.S. military forces is maintaining a safe and secure environment through conducting security patrols in urban areas and in the countryside through their sector.

2002 *Bosnia.* On January 21, 2002, President George W. Bush reported to Congress, "consistent with the War Powers Resolution," that about 3,100 combat-equipped U.S. Armed Forces continued to be deployed in Bosnia-Herzegovina, and other regional states as part of the NATO-led Stabilization Force (SFOR). Most American forces were based at Tuzla in Bosnia. About 500 others were based in Hungary, Croatia, and Italy, providing logistical and other support.

2002 *East Timor.* On February 28, 2002, President George W. Bush reported to Congress, "consistent with the War Powers Resolution," that U. S. Armed Forces were continuing to support the United Nations peacekeeping effort in East Timor aimed at providing security and maintaining law and order in East Timor, coordinating delivery of humanitarian assistance, and helping establish the basis for self-government in East Timor. The United States currently has three military observers attached to the United Nations Transitional Administration in East Timor (UNTAET). The United States also has a separate military presence, the U.S. Support Group East Timor (USGET), comprised of approximately 10 U.S. personnel, including a security detachment, which "facilitates and coordinates" U.S. military activities in East Timor, as well as a rotational presence of U.S. forces through temporary deployments to East Timor. The President stated that U.S. forces would continue a presence through 2002. The President noted his objective was to gradually reduce the "rotational presence operations," and to redeploy USGET personnel, as circumstances permitted.

2002 *Terrorism threat.* On March 20, 2002, President George W. Bush reported to Congress, "consistent with the War Powers Resolution,"on U.S. efforts in the "global war on Terrorism." He noted that the "heart of the al-Qaeda training capability" had been "seriously degraded," and that the remainder of the Taliban and the al-Qaeda fighters were being "actively pursued and engaged by the U.S., coalition and Afghan forces." The U.S. was also conducting "maritime interception operations...to locate and detain suspected al-Qaeda or Taliban leadership fleeing Afghanistan by sea." At the Philippine Government's invitation, the President had ordered deployed "combat-equipped and combat support forces to train with, advise, and assist" the Philippines' Armed Forces in enhancing their "existing counterterrorist capabilities." The strength of U.S. military forces working with the Philippines was projected to be 600 personnel. The President noted that he was "assessing options" for assisting other nations, including Georgia and Yemen, in enhancing their "counterterrorism capabilities, including training and equipping their armed forces." He stated that U.S. combat-equipped and combat support forces would be necessary for these efforts, if undertaken.

2002 *Yugoslavia/Kosovo.* On May 17, 2002, President George W. Bush reported to Congress, "consistent with the War Powers

Resolution," that the U.S. military was continuing to support peacekeeping efforts of the NATO-led international security force in Kosovo (KFOR). He noted that the current U.S. contribution was about 5,100 military personnel, and an additional 468 personnel in Macedonia; with an occasional presence in Albania and Greece.

2002 *Bosnia.* On July 22, 2002, President George W. Bush reported to Congress, "consistent with the War Powers Resolution," that the U.S. military was continuing to support peacekeeping efforts of the NATO-led Stabilization Force (SFOR) in Bosnia-Herzegovina and other regional states. He noted that the current U.S. contribution was "approximately 2,400 personnel." Most U.S. forces in Bosnia-Herzegovina are assigned to the Multinational Division, North headquartered in Tuzla. An additional 60 U.S. military personnel are deployed to Hungary and Croatia to provide logistical and other support.

2002 *Terrorism threat.* On September 20, 2002, President Bush reported to Congress "consistent with the War Powers Resolution," that U.S. "combat-equipped and combat support forces" have been deployed to the Philippines since January 2002 to train with, assist and advise the Philippines' Armed Forces in enhancing their "counterterrorist capabilities." He added that U.S. forces were conducting maritime interception operations in the Central and European Command areas to combat movement, arming or financing of "international terrorists." He also noted that U.S. combat personnel had been deployed to Georgia and Yemen to help enhance the "counterterrorist capabilities" of their armed forces.

2002 *Cote d'Ivoire.* On September 26, 2002, President Bush reported to Congress "consistent with the War Powers Resolution," that in response to a rebellion in Cote d'Ivoire that he had on September 25, 2002 sent U.S. military personnel into Cote d'Ivoire to assist in the evacuation of American citizens and third country nationals from the city of Bouake; and otherwise assist in other evacuations as necessary.

2002 *Yugoslavia/Kosovo.* On November 15, 2002, the President reported to Congress "consistent with the War Powers Resolution" that the U.S. was continuing to deploy combat equipped military personnel as part of the NATO-led international security force in Kosovo (KFOR). Currently there are approximately 4,350 U.S. military personnel in Kosovo, with an additional 266 military personnel in Macedonia. The United States also has an occasional presence in Albania and Greece, associated with the KFOR mission.

2003 *Bosnia.* On January 21, 2003, President George W. Bush reported to Congress, "consistent with the War Powers Resolution," that about 1,800 U.S. Armed Forces personnel continued to be deployed in Bosnia-Herzegovina, and other regional states as part of the NATO-led Stabilization Force (SFOR).Most were based at Tuzla in Bosnia. About 80 others were based in Hungary and Croatia, providing logistical and other support.

2003 *Terrorism threat.* On March 20, 2003, President Bush reported to Congress, "consistent with the War Powers Resolution," as well as P.L. 107-40, and "pursuant to" his authority as Commander-in-Chief, that he had continued a number of U.S. military operations globally in the war against terrorism. These military operations included ongoing U.S. actions against al-Qaeda fighters in Afghanistan; collaborative anti-terror operations with forces of Pakistan in the Pakistan/Afghanistan border area; "maritime interception operations on the high seas" in areas of responsibility of the Central and European Commands to prevent terrorist movement and other activities; and military support for the armed forces of Georgia and Yemen in counter-terrorism operations.

2003 *Iraq War.* On March 21, 2003, President Bush reported to Congress, "consistent with the War Powers Resolution," as well as P.L. 102-1 and P.L. 107-243, and "pursuant to" his authority as Commander-in-Chief, that he had "directed U.S. Armed Forces, operating with other coalition forces, to commence operations on March 19, 2003, against Iraq." He further stated that it was not possible to know at present the duration of active combat operations or the scope necessary to accomplish the goals of the operation "to disarm Iraq in pursuit of peace, stability, and security both in the Gulf region and in the United States."

2003 *Yugoslavia/Kosovo.* On May 14, 2003, President Bush reported to Congress, "consistent with the War Powers Resolution," that combat-equipped U.S. military personnel continued to be deployed as part of the NATO-led international security force in Kosovo (KFOR). He noted that about 2,250 U.S. military personnel were deployed in Kosovo, and additional military personnel operated, on occasion, from Macedonia, Albania, and Greece in support of KFOR operations.

2003 *Liberia.* On June 9, 2003, President Bush reported to Congress, "consistent with the War Powers Resolution," that on June 8 he had sent about 35 combat-equipped U.S. military personnel into Monrovia, Liberia, to augment U.S. Embassy security forces, to aid in the possible evacuation of U.S. citizens if necessary. The President also noted that he had sent about 34 combat-equipped U.S. military personnel to help secure the U.S. Embassy in Nouakchott, Mauritania, and to assist in evacuation of American citizens if required. They were expected to arrive at the U.S. embassy by June 10, 2003. Back-up and support personnel were sent to Dakar, Senegal, to aid in any necessary evacuation from either Liberia or Mauritania.

2003 *Bosnia.* On July 22, 2003, President Bush reported to Congress, "consistent with the War Powers Resolution," that the United States continued to provide about 1,800 combat-equipped military personnel in Bosnia-Herzegovina in support of NATO's Stabilization Force (SFOR) and its peacekeeping efforts in this country.

2003 *Liberia.* On August 13, 2003, President Bush reported to Congress, "consistent with the War Powers Resolution," that in response to conditions in Liberia, on August 11, 2003, he had authorized about 4,350 U.S. combat-equipped military personnel to enter Liberian territorial waters in support of U.N. and West African States efforts to restore order and provide humanitarian assistance in Liberia.

2003 *Terrorism threat.* On September 19, 2003, President Bush reported to Congress "consistent with the War Powers Resolution," that U.S. "combat-equipped and combat support forces" continue to be deployed at a number of locations around the world as part of U.S. anti-terrorism efforts. American forces support anti-terrorism efforts in the Philippines, and maritime interception operations continue on the high seas in the Central, European, and Pacific Command areas of responsibility, to "prevent the movement, arming, or financing of international terrorists." He also noted that "U.S. combat equipped and support forces" had been deployed to Georgia and Djibouti to help in enhancing their "counterterrorist capabilities."

2003 *Yugoslavia/Kosovo.* On November 14, 2003, the President reported to Congress "consistent with the War Powers Resolution" that the United States was continuing to deploy combat equipped military personnel as part of the NATO-led international security force in Kosovo (KFOR). Currently there are approximately 2,100 U.S. military personnel in Kosovo, with additional American military personnel operating out of Macedonia, Albania and Greece, in support of KFOR operations.

2004 *Bosnia.* On January 22, 2004, the President reported to Congress "consistent with the War Powers Resolution" that the United States was continuing to deploy combat equipped military personnel Bosnia and Herzegovina in support of NATO's Stabilization Force (SFOR) and its peacekeeping efforts in this country. About 1,800 U.S. personnel are participating.

2004 *Haiti.* On February 25, 2004, the President reported to Congress "consistent with the War Powers Resolution" that, on February 23, he had sent a combat-equipped "security force" of about "55 U.S. military personnel from the U.S. Joint Forces Command" to Port-au- Prince, Haiti to augment the U.S. Embassy security forces there and to protect American citizens and property in light of the instability created by the armed rebellion in Haiti.

2004 *Haiti.* On March 2, 2004, the President reported to Congress "consistent with the War Powers Resolution" that on February 29 he had sent about "200 additional U.S. combat-equipped, military personnel from the U.S. Joint Forces Command" to Port-au-Prince, Haiti for a variety of purposes, including preparing the way for a U.N. Multinational Interim Force, and otherwise supporting U.N. Security Council Resolution 1529 (2004).

2004 *Terrorism/Bosnia and Haiti.* On March 20, 2004, the President reported to Congress "consistent with the War Powers Resolution," a consolidated report giving details of multiple on-going United States military deployments and operations "in support of the global war on terrorism (including in Afghanistan)," as well as operations in Bosnia and Herzegovina,

Kosovo, and Haiti. In this report, the President noted that U.S. anti-terror related activities were underway in Georgia, Djibouti, Kenya, Ethiopia, Yemen, and Eritrea. He further noted that U.S. combat-equipped military personnel continued to be deployed in Kosovo as part of the NATO-led KFOR (1,900 personnel); in Bosnia and Herzegovina as part of the NATO-led SFOR (about 1,100 personnel); and approximately 1,800 military personnel were deployed in Haiti as part of the U.N. Multinational Interim Force.

2004 *Terrorism threat/Horn of Africa/Kosovo/Bosnia/Iraq.* On November 4, 2004, the President sent to Congress, "consistent with the War Powers Resolution," a consolidated report giving details of multiple ongoing United States military deployments and operations "in support of the global war on terrorism." These deployments, support or military operations include activities in Afghanistan, Djibouti, as well as Kenya, Ethiopia, Eritrea, Bosnia and Herzegovina, and Kosovo. In this report, the President noted that U.S. anti-terror related activities were underway in Djibouti, Kenya, Ethiopia, Yemen, and Eritrea. He further noted that U.S. combat-equipped military personnel continued to be deployed in Kosovo as part of the NATO- led KFOR (1,800 personnel); and in Bosnia and Herzegovina as part of the NATO-led SFOR (about 1,000 personnel). Meanwhile, he stated that the United States continued to deploy more than 135,000 military personnel in Iraq.

2005 *Terrorism threat/Horn of Africa/Kosovo/Bosnia.* On May 20, 2005, the President sent to Congress "consistent with the War Powers Resolution," a consolidated report giving details of multiple ongoing United States military deployments and operations "in support of the global war on terrorism," as well as operations in Iraq, where about 139,000 U.S. military personnel were deployed. U.S. forces are also deployed in Kenya, Ethiopia, Yemen, Eritrea, and Djibouti assisting in "enhancing counter-terrorism capabilities" of these nations. The President further noted that U.S. combat-equipped military personnel continued to be deployed in Kosovo as part of the NATO-led KFOR (1,700 personnel). Approximately 235 U.S. personnel are also deployed in Bosnia and Herzegovina as part of the NATO Headquarters-Sarajevo who assist in defense reform and perform operational tasks, such as counter-terrorism and supporting the International Criminal Court for the Former Yugoslavia.

2005 *Terrorism threat/Horn of Africa/Kosovo/Bosnia/Iraq.* On December 7, 2005, the President sent to Congress "consistent" with the War Powers Resolution, a consolidated report giving details of multiple ongoing United States military deployments and operations "in support of the global war on terrorism," and in support of the Multinational Force in Iraq, where about 160,000 U.S. military personnel were deployed. U.S. forces were also deployed in the Horn of Africa region — Kenya, Ethiopia, Yemen, and Djibouti — assisting in "enhancing counter-terrorism capabilities" of these nations. The President further noted that U.S. combat-equipped military personnel continued to be deployed in Kosovo as part of the NATO-led KFOR (1,700 personnel). Approximately 220 U.S. personnel were also deployed in Bosnia and Herzegovina as part of the NATO Headquarters-Sarajevo who assist in defense reform and perform operational tasks, such as "counter-terrorism and supporting the International Criminal Court for the Former Yugoslavia."

2006 *Terrorism threat/Kosovo/Bosnia/Iraq.* On June 15, 2006, the President sent to Congress "consistent" with the War Powers Resolution, a consolidated report giving details of multiple ongoing United States military deployments and operations "in support of the war on terror," and in Kosovo, Bosnia and Herzegovina, and as part of the Multinational Force (MNF) in Iraq. About 131,000 military personnel were deployed in Iraq. U.S. forces were also deployed in the Horn of Africa region, and in Djibouti to support necessary operations against al-Qaida and other international terrorists operating in the region. U.S. military personnel continue to support the NATO- led Kosovo Force (KFOR). The U.S. contribution to KFOR was about 1,700 military personnel. The NATO Headquarters-Sarajevo was established in November 22, 2004 as a successor to its stabilization operations in Bosnia-Herzegovina to continue to assist in implementing the peace agreement. Approximately 250 U.S. personnel were assigned to the NATO Headquarters-Sarajevo to assist in defense reform and perform operational tasks, such as "counter-terrorism and supporting the International Criminal Court for the Former Yugoslavia."

2006 *Lebanon.* On July 18, 2006, the President reported to Congress "consistent" with the War Powers Resolution, that in response to the security threat posed in Lebanon to U.S. Embassy personnel and citizens and designated third country personnel," he had deployed combat-equipped military helicopters and military personnel to Beirut to assist in the departure of the persons under threat from Lebanon. The President noted that additional combat-equipped U.S. military forces may be deployed "to Lebanon, Cyprus and other locations, as necessary." to assist further departures of persons from Lebanon and to provide security. He further stated that once the threat to U.S. citizens and property has ended, the U.S. military forces would redeploy.

2006 *Terrorism threat/Horn of Africa/Kosovo/Bosnia.* On December 15, 2006, the President sent to Congress "consistent" with the War Powers Resolution, a consolidated report giving details of multiple ongoing United States military deployments and operations "in support of the war on terror," in Kosovo, Bosnia and Herzegovina, and as part of the Multinational Force (MNF) in Iraq. About 134,000 military personnel are deployed in Iraq. U.S. forces were also deployed in the Horn of Africa region, and in Djibouti to support necessary operations against al-Qaida and other international terrorists operating in the region, including Yemen. U.S. military personnel continue to support the NATO-led Kosovo Force (KFOR). The U.S. contribution to KFOR was about 1,700 military personnel. The NATO Headquarters-Sarajevo was established in November 22, 2004 as a successor to its stabilization operations in Bosnia- Herzegovina to continue to assist in implementing the peace agreement. Approximately 100 U.S. personnel were assigned to the NATO Headquarters-Sarajevo to assist in defense reform and perform operational tasks, such as "counter-terrorism and supporting the International Criminal Court for the Former Yugoslavia."

2007 *Terrorism threat/Kosovo/Afghanistan.* On June 15, 2007, the President sent to Congress "consistent" with the War Powers Resolution, a consolidated report giving details of ongoing United States military deployments and operations "in support of the war on terror,"and in support of the NATO-led Kosovo Force (KFOR). The President reported that various U.S. "combat-equipped and combat- support forces" were deployed to "a number of locations in the Central, Pacific, European (KFOR), and Southern Command areas of operation" and were engaged in combat operations against al-Qaida terrorists and their supporters. The U.S. is currently "pursuing and engaging remnant al-Qaida and Taliban fighters in Afghanistan." U.S. forces in Afghanistan currently total approximately 25,945. Of this total, "approximately 14,340 are assigned to the International Security Assistance Force (ISAF) in Afghanistan." The U.S. military continues to support peacekeeping operations in Kosovo, specifically, the NATO-led Kosovo Force (KFOR). Currently, the U.S. contribution to KFOR in Kosovo is approximately 1,584 military personnel. *Terrorism threat/Kosovo/Afghanistan.* On December 14, 2007, the President sent to Congress "consistent with the War Powers Resolution," a consolidated report giving details of ongoing United States military deployments and operations "in support of the war on terror,"and in support of the NATO-led Kosovo Force (KFOR). The resident reported that various U.S. "combat-equipped and combat- support forces" were deployed to "a number of locations in the Central, Pacific, European, and Southern Command areas of operation" and were engaged in combat operations against al-Qaida terrorists and their supporters. The U.S. is currently "pursuing and engaging remnant al-Qaida and Taliban fighters in Afghanistan." U.S. forces in Afghanistan currently total approximately 25,900. Of this total, "approximately 15,180 are assigned to the International Security Assistance Force (ISAF) in Afghanistan." The U.S. military continues to support peacekeeping operations in Kosovo, specifically, the NATO-led Kosovo Force (KFOR). Currently, the U.S. contribution to KFOR in Kosovo is approximately 1,498 military personnel.

INDEX

C

D

E

F

G

N

O

P

Q

R

S

T

U

V

W

Y